What I've Stolen,
What I've Earned

Also by Sherman Alexie

What I've Stolen, What I've Earned

Sherman Alexie

Hanging Loose Press
Brooklyn, New York

Published by Hanging Loose Press, 231 Wyckoff Street, Brooklyn, New York 11217-2208. All rights reserved. No part of this book may be reproduced without the publisher's written permission, except for brief quotations in reviews.

www.hangingloosepress.com

Printed in the United States of America
10 9 8 7 6 5 4 3 2 1

Cover photograph by Frank Cusack

Cover design by Marie Carter

Acknowledgments: Some of these poems have previously appeared in 6 x 6, Agni, Alaska Quarterly Review, American Poetry Review, Beloit Poetry Journal, Cincinnati Review, Colorado Review, Contrary, Court Green, Denver Quarterly, Hanging Loose, Harpur Palate, The Journal, Knockout, New Madrid, Ninth Letter, The Normal School, Orion, Pank, Redivider, Slipstream, Smartish Pace, Specs, The Stranger, Summerset Review, Tin House, True Hoop, Unsplendid, Zone 3

ISBN: 978-1934909-32-4 (paperback)
ISBN: 978-1934909-37-9 (hardcover)

Library of Congress cataloging-in-progress number available on request.

Contents

III Odes to Now

IV My Indian Names

For Diane, Joseph, and David, my favorite trinity

I Crazy Horse Boulevard

Crazy Horse Boulevard

1.

During his lifetime, my big brother has chosen and been chosen by six best friends.

Five of them have died in car wrecks.

In Indian theology, there are Four Directions: East, West, North, and South. Sounds expansive, I guess, but it's really limited. What if I walked south for ten feet and then suddenly turned west and walked for two thousand miles? How would one theologically measure the difference between those two paths? Would those ten thousand miles west be more sacred than those ten feet south? And what if I walked in a northwestern direction? Come on, come on, people, there are a hell of a lot more than Four Directions, even in a metaphorical sense.

And, really, there are maybe three Indians in the whole country who can say "The Four Directions" without secretly giggling.

This might be only the second time that somebody has put "Indians" and "giggling" in the same sentence.

I've only been to the funeral for one of my brother's best friends. It was a highly traditional ceremony, so the mournful Indians spent a lot of time giggling.

2.

What if one is not the loneliest number?

What if two is actually the loneliest number? After all, how many times have you had your heart truly broken by a large group of people? You really have to be most wary of the other half of the couples you've created. Or been born into.

My friend says she's only been in romantic love three times. My other friend says he falls in love three times during his commute to work.

At the present moment, I have four dollars in my wallet. What if this were my only wealth? At times in my younger life, my entire wealth was less than four dollars. When it comes to love, is there a difference between four dollars and four million dollars? What did Lear say to his daughter Cordelia, who truly loved him but was too tongue-tied to say anything other than "nothing" when he asked her what praise she had for him? He said, "Nothing will come of nothing." That fucker Lear disinherited his daughter because she was less articulate than her sisters. How's that for love?

I've served on the Board of Trustees for five different charitable organizations. I've lost count of the number of times a rich person would only give money if his or her name were publicly printed in bold type. Rich people want buildings to be named after them. Rich people want cities to be named for them. I think the saddest people in the world are rich. Maybe one billion is the loneliest number.

I worry that my big brother will soon lose the sixth best friend of his lifetime. I worry that my brother will outlive everybody. I worry that he'll be the last person on earth and spend his life wandering among innumerable gravestones. And I've just decided that the only structure that should bear anybody's name is a gravestone.

3.

I bet you all the money in my wallet that my brother is carrying about six dollars in his pocket. That would, indeed, be his entire wealth.

I love my big brother. I love my big brother. I love my big brother. I love my big brother. I love my big brother.

The fourth word in my copy of Webster's Ninth New Collegiate Dictionary (which I received in 1985 as a high school graduation gift from the Franson family) is *aardwolf*, "a maned, striped mammal of southern and eastern Africa that resembles the related hyenas and feeds chiefly on carrion and insects." Have you ever heard of the aardwolf? It sounds like some mythical creature straight out of Dungeons & Dragons. I'm afraid to search for more information about the thing, though, because I'm sure it's extinct. One can't talk about Indians and death and genocide without magically discovering other dead and dying species.

Okay, I wait about three minutes before I type "aardwolf" into my search engine. And, hooray, the aardwolf is still alive! Though it's the "only surviving species of the subfamily Protelinae" (whatever that is). And what's more, this animal is a genocidal eater. According to Wikipedia, the aardwolf feeds mainly on termites and can eat more than 200,000 in a single night. Holy shit! Right now, in Africa, there's a termite shaman telling his people, "The aardwolf comes at us from every fucking direction."

It was around closing time, 2 a.m, when I saw Gail Franson in a grocery store in Spokane. This was maybe two years after I graduated from high school. Gail was a few years older, my big brother's age, and I'd always had a mad crush on her. And there she was. "Hey, that's Gail," I said to my big brother, who was stealing and eating food from the fruit department. He didn't care. But I shouted, "Hey, Gail, I love you! You have great legs!" She blushed and turned away. It probably doesn't surprise you that I haven't seen her since that moment. And, oh, just to remind you: It was Gail's family who gave me that dictionary as a graduation present. What does it say about me that I've kept this outmoded dictionary for twenty-six years?

Like my big brother, I have also had six best friends in my life. All of them are still alive, though I only have contact with one of them.

4.

Who are the six greatest human beings who have ever lived? I bet you that most men would list six other men. And most women would list three women and three men.

Off the top of my head: Crazy Horse. Martin Luther King, Jr. Michelangelo. Emily Dickinson. The person who invented the smallpox vaccine. That's five. I'll leave the last spot open because I'm sure I've forgotten somebody obvious. Four men and one woman. What does that say about me? Of course, I'm just assuming the inventor of the smallpox vaccine was a man. Isn't that sexist? Well, I look it up and discover that Edward Jenner invented the smallpox vaccine in 1796. What? Do you know how many Indians died from smallpox after 1796? Millions! Just when you think the United States couldn't have been more genocidal, you discover more evidence.

I'm guessing there are four kids in each of my sons' classes who haven't been immunized against mumps, measles, and rubella. If my sons, Indian as they are, contract some preventable disease from those organic, free-range white children and die, will it be legal for me to scalp and slaughter their white parents?

Three arrows: One in the head, one in the heart, and one in the crotch.

Two thoughts: Is there such a thing as Crazy Horse Boulevard? And if so, have white people built big houses there? In Seattle, when white folks first gentrified this neighborhood, they built big houses on Martin Luther King, Jr. Boulevard, but they turned the front doors of their homes so their street addresses would not be on MLK, Jr. Blvd.

Among my immediate family, I'm the only one who doesn't live on the reservation. What does that say about me?

5.

Aardvark is the first word in my ancient dictionary. But aardwolf is a far more interesting word, animal, and concept. That's how poems get written.

Last week, my sister sent me two questions from her final exam in Native American Literature 101. Yes, my sister is studying my books in her class. And yes, she's unsure of the answers. I don't even want to think about the ramifications of this. Sometimes the poem doesn't need to be written.

Three ironies: I just included the discussion of what should be unwritten in this poem. Most of the people who read this poem will be white people. This poem doesn't use any form of rhyme or meter, so it's called free verse. Yes, an Indian is using free verse to write about that rural concentration camp known as a reservation.

Okay, I think that was four ironies.

My big brother has helped carry five coffins from hearse to Longhouse, Longhouse back to hearse, hearse to graveside, and graveside to grave.

Here's a game: Grab a six-sided die. No, roll one red die and one white die together. Read the red die first and refer to the corresponding section of this poem; then read the white die and refer to the corresponding stanza of each numbered section. For example, if you rolled a red 4 and a white 6, you'd be reading this stanza. Now, roll the dice thirty-six times and reorder this poem. Do this as many times as you wish. No matter what happens, remember that my big brother, though he may not admit it, fully expects to bury his sixth best friend in the very near future.

6.

In the first six drafts of this poem, I placed the previous stanza at the end of the poem. But, for some ineffable reason, I decided that it wasn't correct. But who knows? When you write by instinct, you're going to get a whole lot of shit wrong.

We all live by instinct. We all live by instinct. We all live by instinct. We all live by instinct. We all live by instinct.

Ineffable. Ineffable. Ineffable. Ineffable.

My big brother's holy trinity: Beer, pizza, and death songs.

Ah, big brother, when was the last time you and I sang together? What happened to our duet?

I've only got one birthmark. It's a heart-shaped mole on my right arm. It's next to a comet-shaped burn scar. What does this say about me?

The Native American Dictionary, Page 1

Indian giver, *n*. Popularly thought of as an Indian who gives and then takes back, but actually someone (usually a Caucasian male) who gives to Indians and then steals it back.

First love, *n*. That Jingle Dancer (Search: Jingle Dancer on YouTube). It's always, always, always a Jingle Dancer. And she, like every other Indian woman in the world, fell in love with a Grass Dancing Indian boy from Montana instead of you, and broke your heart. Additionally, if you close your eyes, the gorgeous roar of one thousand Jingle Dancers sounds like your heart falling off a ten-story drum and crashing into a fry bread truck.

Cell phone, *n*. A multi-functional communication device that is not, according to most studies, hazardous to human health. In Indian parlance, when one signs a contract with a cell phone provider, one is signing a "peace treaty." See: Thalidomide.

Powwow, *n*. An event where middle-class white people come to watch and take photos of dancing Indians. Also, a meeting during which rich white people discuss the ways in which they can steal land from Indians.

Indian Health Service, *v*. A threat delivered to Indian children as a disciplinary method, e.g., "If you don't behave, I'm going to Indian Health Service you."

Apple, n. A derogatory term (red on the outside, white on the inside) for an Indian who usually has a college education, a job, and at least 90% of his or her teeth.

Republican, *n*. One who has, in the past, lied to Indians. Also, one who is currently lying to Indians. Also, one who will, in the future, lie to Indians. *See*: Democrat.

Survival, *n*. Holy, holy, holy, cousin, that's just what Indians do.

Disguise

If I ever decide to rob a bank,
I'll wear full war dance regalia.
Nobody will believe that an Indian
Would so obviously hide
Behind all those feathers and war paint.

Family Memoir

We carried the furniture out of the burning house—
it was a blistered-finger chore—
And then hurried all of the chairs, sofas, and beds
into the burning house next door.

Good Hair

Hey, Indian boy, why (why!) did you slice off your braids?
Do you grieve their loss? Have you thought twice about your braids?

With that long, black hair, you looked overtly Indian.
If vanity equals vice, then does vice equal braids?

Are you warrior-pretend? Are you horseback-never?
Was your drum-less, drum-less life disguised by your braids?

Hey, Indian boy, why (why!) did you slice off your braids?
You have school-age kids, so did head lice invade your braids?

Were the scissors impulsive or inevitable?
Did you arrive home and say, "Surprise, I cut my braids"?

Do you miss the strange women who loved to touch your hair?
Do you miss being eroticized because of your braids?

Hey, Indian boy, why (why!) did you slice off your braids?
Did you weep or laugh when you said goodbye to your braids?

Did you donate your hair for somebody's chemo wig?
Is there a cancer kid who thrives because of your braids?

Did you, peace chief, give your hair to an orphaned sparrow?
Is there a bald eagle that flies because of your braids?

Hey, Indian boy, why (why!) did you slice off your braids?
Was it worth it? Did you profit? What's the price of braids?

Did you cut your hair after your sister's funeral?
Was it self-flagellation? Did you chastise your braids?

Have your tribe and clan cut-hair-mourned since their creation?
Did you, ceremony-dumb, improvise with your braids?

Hey, Indian boy, why (why!) did you slice off your braids?
Was it a violent act? Did you despise your braids?

Did you cut your hair after booze murdered your father?
When he was buried, did you baptize him with your braids?

Did you weave your hair with your siblings' and mother's hair,
And pray that your father grave-awakes and climbs your braids?

Powwow Ghazal

Can you hear the drums? Can you hear the drums?
Tonight, the reservation is aflame with drums.

Who's that drum group? They're good, but they're kids.
They have no idea how their lives will change with drums.

And what about those other drummers over there? O, they're old-school.
They're everybody's elders. They've gone grey with drums.

O, listen to that singer! He's equal parts joy and hurt.
His hands and vocal cords are bloodstained with drums.

Damn, look at that fancydancer spin in circles.
She's weeping! The girl is going insane with drums.

Who's the head man dancer? He's been sober for ten years.
Now he only gets drunk, stoned, and dazed with drums.

Who's the head woman dancer? That's a grandmother.
She speaks in sermons. She offers us grace with drums.

That shawl dancer, ah, she's a reservation beauty.
Talk to her, cousin, because you can get laid with drums.

That nostalgic Indian is wearing blue suede shoes.
He's the Indian Elvis, mixing his pomade with drums.

Hey, look at that tribal cop with a shiny badge and gun.
She wants to solve a crime. She's Sam Spade with drums.

But don't forget that powwows can be dangerous, too.
You better duck, or get punched in the face with drums.

Do you have a question? It can be answered here.
There is nothing that can't be explained with drums.

No, I'm lying. Indians are glorious deceivers.
We love to obscure, obfuscate, and exaggerate with drums.

During powwow, even God wants to sing and dance,
So God makes thunder, lightning, and rain with drums.

Nobody has gone to bed yet. We've been awake for days.
Sometimes I think that every Indian is made of drums.

After the Powwow, the Fancydancers Need to Get Clean

We Indian boys showered in the rain,
And used our own braids to scrub the stains.

Happy Holidays!

1.

Indians love fireworks.

We make millions selling illegal ones to white folks.

Well, not millions for each of us, but you know what I mean.

A working definition of tolerance: When Indians make money from white
    folks celebrating their independence.

Ever have a bottle rocket fight? I've got a burn scar on my left thumb.

Reservation rumor: an M-80 firecracker was as powerful as a ¼ stick
    of dynamite. Wasn't true, but we pretended it was true when we
    threw them into ant piles.

2.

White eggs come from white chickens; brown eggs come from
    brown chickens.

Have you ever hidden an egg in your home for the Easter hunt, and
    then been unable to find it for days or even weeks afterward?
    A few years ago, we hid an ostrich egg (an ostrich egg!) in our living
    room and never found it. It still hasn't gone bad enough to find it
    by smell. Every so often, I look for it.

When I was a child, I cracked open a bright green painted egg
    and discovered a chicken fetus inside.

My high school girlfriend raised chickens. "About every fifty eggs or so,"
    she said, "you drop a fetus into the frying pan."

Sunnyside up, with lots of Tabasco, and four triangles of buttered toast.

White Jesus comes from white people; brown Jesus comes from
    brown people.

3.

Pine trees, pine trees, pine trees.

My family didn't have indoor plumbing until I was seven years old.

We lived in an epic, and gorgeous, pine forest.

Therefore, pine tree = poverty.

Therefore, poverty = epic and gorgeous.

There is some sort of bad logic in this, but I don't remember the name for it.

4.

I am asked this question at least a dozen times every year: "Do Indians
    celebrate Thanksgiving?"

That's like asking: "Do Jewish people celebrate Oktoberfest?"

The answer is: "Yes, Indians celebrate Thanksgiving."

I just emailed a Jewish friend to ask about her feelings on Oktoberfest,
    and she wrote, "Never thought about it. No way I'd buy
    a BMW, though."

The best thing about humans: Our ability to forgive. The second
    best thing: Grudges.

About 70% white meat and 30% dark, with canned cranberry sauce. And
    no, I don't care how good your homemade cranberry sauce is.

5.

On a New Year's Eve when I was five or six, my mother, drunk
        for the very last time, punched an older Indian woman in the face.

My mother hates it when I write about this.

Once a friend told me, "I heard your mother singing in church today. It
        sounded like the river at night." A nine-year-old Indian boy said
        that about my mother! Where is that Indian boy? Did the poet
        in him survive?

I am vaguely Catholic, so for the rest of this poem I will fast.

My wife, two sons, and I celebrate the New Year by drinking root beer
        floats. I hereby establish the root beer float as the official Native
        American New Year's Eve drink. It should be the only drink
        allowed for Indians on New Year's.

Ain't gonna happen.

I want to combine Catholic Lent and the Jewish Day of Atonement,
        and begin each year with six weeks of apologies.

6.

Dear Ants that I slaughtered with M-80 fireworks, I am sorry for my rage.

Dear Chickens-to-Be that I dropped into frying pans, I am sorry for my hunger.

Dear Family Outhouse, I am sorry that I failed to recognize your primitive beauty.

Dear Enemies, real and imagined, I am sorry for my grudges.

Dear Mother, For having written so many poems and stories about you,
I am sorry.

Dear Universe, I am sorry for all the times that I believed myself to be
the sun around which all of these planets whirl.

Monosonnet for the Matriarchy, Interrupted

When
A
Woman
Asks
You
To
Owl
Dance

(O, O, O, O, the owl dance, two steps forward, one step back, O, O, O, O,
listen to the drummers attack that drum, O, O, O, O, if a woman asks you to
owl dance, you have to accept her offer, O, O, O, O, but if you still have the
nerve to decline, then you must pay her what she wants, O, O, O, O, give her
some money, honey, fill her coffers, O, O, O, O, and then you have to stand
in front of the entire powwow and tell everybody exactly why and how you
refused her, O, O, O, O, and if you refuse to detail your refusal, you will be
named and shamed out of the powwow, O, O, O, O, but, mister, why would
you want to say no to your sister, O, O, O, O, but, brother, why would you
want to say no to your mother, O, O, O, O, all of these women are your sisters
and mothers, O, O, O, O, they're somebody's sisters and mothers, so, mister,
so, brother, dance with the women, dance with the women, dance with the
women, dance with the women, they're everybody's sisters and mothers),

You
Should
Always
Honor
The
Chance.

Hummingbird

1.

Small bird, pollinating bird, impossible bird,
You are the only one that can fly in reverse.
Your heart beats 1,200 times a minute. Absurd!

But I find it more absurd to learn that the Aztecs
Worshipped you as an icon of war and sex
(But not of fatherhood: Males never keep nest).

So tell me, winged one, are you more afraid
       of birth or death?

2.

Hey, little man, named after the hummingbird,
You lived your whole damn life in reverse.
You shot yourself twice before you died. Absurd!

They say basketball was a deadly game for the Aztecs.
If so, then you were the point guard of war and sex
(But not of fatherhood: You never kept nest).

So tell me, cousin, what do you regret more: your birth or your death?

Sonnet, with Slot Machines

1. Gambling is traditional. 2. So is the sacrificial murder of mammals, but who is going to start that up again? 3. Well, folks find ritually slaughtered animals all the time, so perhaps the question should be: Who among us has stopped that shit? 4. The vegans would insist that all carnivorous humans are ritual murderers. 5. Those vegans are not wrong, I think, as I eat my medium-rare steak. 6. So what about Indian casinos? 7. It's all about economic sovereignty for indigenous peoples! 8. Well sure, but can't a slot machine ritually murder the gambler's soul? 9. The Indian woman, defending her tribe's casino, says, "The average patron only gambles $42 a night." 10. Well, stating the obvious, that's $1,260 a month. 11. And $15,120 a year. 12. O, trust me, I'm trying to find the poetry in these numbers. 13. Wait, here it is, make the "b" silent, and pronounce it *"nummer,"* as in "remove sensation, especially as a result of cold or anesthesia, as in "remove emotion." 14. If you punch a kid once, then he'll cry. If you punch a kid once an hour for a year, then he'll learn how to make the fists feel like flowers.

What Happened

We remember catching
Praying mantises
During our reservation childhood
And putting two,
Like primordial, gladiator jocks,
Into a shoebox
For a battle.
And, O, we Indian boys
Would shake the death
Rattle
For our favorite
Warrior Mantis.
Remember, this was before
Casinos,
So any reservation
Might as well have been
Atlantis.
We were that far removed
From you
And you
And you.
During those warrior years,
We'd give the most deadly mantises
Fighter names,
Like Blood Thirsty
Or Killer Monk.
But we'd also give them cute
And ironic names,
Like Socks or Smells
Like Skunk.
And we, brother upon
Brother, cheered
As one mantis slaughtered
The other.
We'd give the victorious mantis,

As reward,
One grasshopper
From our hoard
Of living food.
Crude and cruel,
We tore off the hoppers'
Legs and wings
And turned them into
These limbless
Things.
Damn, it was wrong.
So, last week, feeling
Like we'd crashed
Through the ceiling
And concussed our souls,
We discussed our options
And called our mothers
From our homes
In Seattle,
And asked them
If any of the new reservation kids,
Newly cruel,
Also collect, train,
And battle mantises.
"No," our mothers said.
"We haven't seen a praying mantis
In years. We think
They're all dead."
What happened?
What happened?
We remember one mantis—
Captured at night
With a flashlight—
That refused to fight.
In the box, it paused,
Retracted its forelegs
And those alien claws,
Turned its head,

With that heart-shaped face
And red eyes,
And surprise, surprise,
It stared at us.
We swear
It was self-aware
And aware
Of us.
It regarded us.
It judged us.
Then, with great speed,
Its opponent mantis,
Smaller but more aggressive,
Decapitated
The one that would not fight.
Can a mantis
Commit suicide?
Did that mantis crucify
Itself
Because of our sins?
Who knows what
A mantis thinks, if
It thinks at all.
Or if it's all
Reflex
Of hunt and eat and sex.
Jesus, we Indian boys
Were bones broken
Through skin.
We, thin and thinner,
Were raped and pillaged
By time and color
And faith and dozens
Of cousins, and after
Our escape, took
Revenge on the human race
And every last sun
In outer space

By murdering
Hundreds of mantises.
I doubt that we killed enough
To eradicate them
From the rez, but we—
The grandchildren
Of genocide—
Were dedicated
To violence.
And now, a generation
Later, we gather
Every fall to call
Back what we destroyed.
O, we make
A glorious noise.
O, we dance circles
Around a cask
Filled with blood
Or mud,
And we dance
As if we have a chance
To be redeemed.
We Indian boys—
Now un-young and un-pretty—
Relocated
From the reservation
To the city—
Will dance, dance
As compensation.
This is our holy task.
We'll honor the dead
By wearing eagle feathers
And mantis
Masks.

Love Song, with Alcohol

You are a bar fight
Spilling into the streets at noon.
I'm going to leave you.
But not anytime soon.

II   Sonnets, With and Without

Sonnet, with Pride

Inspired by Pride of Baghdad *by Brian K. Vaughan and Niko Henrichon*

1. In 2003, during the Iraq War, a pride of lions escaped from the Baghdad Zoo during an American bombing raid. 2. Confused, injured, unexpectedly free, the lions roamed the streets searching for food and safety. 3. For just a moment, imagine yourself as an Iraqi living in Baghdad. You are running for cover as the U.S. bombers, like metal pterodactyls, roar overhead. You are running for cover as some of your fellow citizens, armed and angry, fire rifles, rocket launchers, and mortars into the sky. You are running for cover as people are dying all around you. It's war, war, war. And then you turn a corner and see a pride of freaking lions advancing on you. 4. Now, imagine yourself as a lion that has never been on a hunt. That has never walked outside of a cage. That has been coddled and fed all of its life. And now your world is exploding all around you. It's war, war, war. And then you turn a corner and see a pride of freaking tanks advancing on you. 5. It's okay to laugh. It's always okay to laugh at tragedy. If lions are capable of laughter, then I'm positive those Baghdad lions were laughing at their predicament. As they watched the city burn and collapse, I'm sure a lioness turned to a lion and said, "So do you still think you're the King of the Jungle?" 6. I don't know if the lions killed anybody as they roamed through the streets. 7. But I'd guess they were too afraid. I'm sure they could only see humans as zookeepers, not food. 8. In any case, the starving lions were eventually shot and killed by U.S. soldiers on patrol. 9. It's a sad and terrible story, yes, but that is war. And war is everywhere. And everywhere there are prides of starving lions wandering the streets. There are prides of starving lions wandering inside your hearts. 10. You might also think that I'm using starving lions as a metaphor for homeless folks, but I'm not. Homeless folks have been used far too often as targets for metaphors. I'm using those starving lions as a simple metaphor for hunger. All of our hunger. 11. Food-hunger. Love-hunger. Faith-hunger. Soul-hunger. 12. Who among us has been not been hungry? Who among us has not been vulnerable? Who among us has not been a starving lion? Who among us has not been a prey animal? Who among us has not been a predator? 13. They say God created humans in God's image. But what if God also created lions in God's image? What if God created hunger in God's image? What if God is hunger? Tell me, how do you pray to hunger? How do you ask for hunger's blessing? How will hunger teach you to forgive? How will hunger teach you how to love? 14. Look out the window. It's all hunger and war. Hunger and war. Hunger and war. And the endless pride of lions.

Monosonnet for Colonialism, Interrupted

Yes,
Colonialism
Created
George
Custer
And
Andrew
Jackson

(who were genocidal maniacs, but without American colonialism we would
not have action-adventure movies like *Die Hard* or the consolations and
desolations of Emily Dickinson. I am a man who loves cinematic gunfire and
American poetry, if not equally, then with parallel passion. In fact, at one point,
I considered writing an action-adventure movie about Emily Dickinson. I
even designed a poster for this movie that has not been written, let alone cast,
shot, or edited. The poster features an actress [think of the latest and greatest
young and muscular American actress] dressed in a tattered white gown while
holding a large automatic pistol at an acute angle to the ground. The movie
is called *Emily*. And the tagline, the little phrase that will sell the movie to
millions, is "Her Life Stood a Loaded Gun." Now, tell me, who wouldn't want
to see that flick? Of course, such a film would never be made, but can you
appreciate the basic principle of the cultural mash-up? Can you appreciate
this improvisational and highly American olio of poetry, film, and comedy?),

But
Colonialism
Also
Created
Miles
Davis.

Sonnet, with Water Cooler

1. 65 million people watched the series finale of *M*A*S*H*. 2. The plot line: Hawkeye, as played by Alan Alda, is in a mental hospital because of a mysterious tragedy during a civilian bus escape he led through dangerous North Korean territory. With enemy forces all around, Hawkeye repeatedly orders a Korean woman to keep her squawking chicken quiet lest it give away their location. After numerous unsuccessful attempts to calm her bird, the woman finally suffocates it. 3. Why would a dead chicken cause such anguish? 4. Well, we learn that Hawkeye had repressed the truth. The woman had not killed a chicken. She'd suffocated her baby because he could not stop crying. 5. One of the most devastating moments in television history. 6. And 65 million people watched it. 65 million! 7. The morning after the show, those 65 million told at least 65 million other people what they had seen. 8. By the end of that workday, I would guess that most of the country knew about the mother who'd killed her baby. 9. How often must a fictional story be repeated before it becomes the truth? 10. How many people heard only fragments of the story and believed that a real woman had suffocated her real baby in order to save her family from a mysterious killer? 11. I'd venture that tens of thousands wept for the baby they'd mistakenly believed was real, and turned fiction into myth. Yes, beauty can be accidental and incidental. 12. Can you imagine what it would take now for hundreds of millions of Americans to discuss the same topic? It would take a real war, or a real revolution that threatens to become a war. 13. But millions of us remember when a fictional war had just as much power as a real one, though a friend of mine, after reading this poem, said, "Real wars are just fictions, too." 14. But, whether it was real or fiction, millions of us remember when we collectively held a wailing baby in our arms and wondered if we could sacrifice its life in order to save one hundred strangers.

Love Sonnet, Constructed by Wikipedia

1. Love is a universal construct related to affinity.

2. Affinity, etymologically, is the opposite of infinity.

3. Love and ego are incompatible.

4. A group of female college students smelled T-shirts that had been worn by male students for two nights, without deodorant, cologne, or scented soaps. Overwhelmingly, the women preferred the odors of men with genomes dissimilar to their own.

5. The human tongue can distinguish only among five distinct qualities of taste, while the nose can distinguish among hundreds of substances, even in minute quantities.

6. Most love songs are addressed directly to the person being admired. Changes in style mean that few songs survive more than fifty years.

7. Vocalization and percussion are the most important aspects of traditional Native American music. Vocalization takes many forms, ranging from solo and choral song to responsorial, unison and multipart singing. Percussion, especially drums and rattles, is common accompaniment to keep the rhythm steady for the singers.

8. If a snake's rattle absorbs enough moisture in wet weather, it will not make noise. Iron rain falls on some planets. There are many factors that go into how long a human can survive without water, and the will to do so is one of them. The inner earth may hold more water—unattainable as of yet—than the seas.

9. The Petrarchan sonnet is a verse form that typically refers to the concept of unattainable love.

10. "I'm So Lonesome I Could Cry" is a song written and recorded by American country music singer-songwriter Hank Williams in 1949. With evocative lyrics, such as the opening lines "Hear that lonesome whip-poor-

will/He sounds too blue to cry," the song has been covered by Johnny Cash, Bob Dylan, Little Richard, Dolly Parton, and Elvis Presley, among many others.

11. Intimacy requires an ability to be participants both separately and together in a relationship. Murray Bowen called this "self-differentiation." It results in a connection in which there is emotional range involving both robust conflict and intense loyalty.

12. The Medal of Honor is bestowed by the United States Congress on members of the United States Armed Forces who distinguish themselves through "conspicuous gallantry and intrepidity at the risk of his or her life above and beyond the call of duty while engaged in an action against an enemy of the Unites States." Due to the nature of its criteria, it is often awarded posthumously (as more than half have been since 1941).

13. In 2006, the latest year studied, Native American men were dying at the highest rate of all people.

14. "Lovers ever run before the clock."

Touch

1.

I want to invent an iPad game where you attempt to become a saint by
virtually replicating the pain of actually becoming a saint.

2.

Using the touch screen, you'll be able to throw yourself into a rose bush and
bloody yourself in the thorns.

3.

You can use your fingertip or a stylus to scratch, scratch, scratch, and scratch
your smallpox scars.

4.

As the audience jeers you, swipe down to kneel for the lions coming to feast
on your loving heart.

5.

You can swipe up on the screen to throw bread into the mouths of hungry
children.

6.

Tap, tap, and tap the screen repeatedly to start the pyre that burns you alive.

7.

Bleeding from the forehead is free, but you'll have to pay 99 cents extra to bleed from your feet and wrists.

8.

Predict the day of your death, and then finger-spin the calendar wheel to see if you are prescient.

9.

I'll try to develop a forgiveness update, but I'm not sure we have the technology for that.

10.

You can choose: Dodge the arrows, or stand still and be martyred.

11.

All of our early advertising will guarantee that you don't have to be Catholic in order to enjoy mystical and/or metaphorical self-flagellation.

12.

Before playing the game, you must fast for three days. We'll install a detector that will test your fingertips for traces of food.

13.

If you die, you can come back to life, of course.

14.

In the final stage, you'll have to pick up Christ and carry him across a river, though you'll find, through some miracle of science and faith, that your iPad will get heavier and heavier with each passing second, until it weighs the same as the whole world.

Hell

1.

In one of his poems, Ron Padgett claims that Dante's real name is Durante. Could this be true?

2.

I won't look it up. I need it to be true.

3.

Ron also claims that he couldn't sleep because he kept equating Dante with Jimmy Durante.

4.

I want to believe that the very thought of Jimmy Durante could prevent sleep. Not because I think Jimmy Durante is that disturbing. I just like to be surprised by other people's obsessions.

5.

For instance, this morning, after I dropped the boys at school, I raced back home because I thought I'd left the stove fires burning. Of course, I'd turned off the flame, but you could not have convinced me of this if I had not seen it for myself. In fact, as I stared at the inert burner, I was still worried that it was burning. Hours later, as I write this poem, I have the intense desire to run into the kitchen and check.

6.

I realize that I wrote a stanza about fire shortly after I wrote a stanza about Dante. I didn't mean to connect my stove (and my obsessive-compulsive disorder) with the Nine Circles of Hell.

7.

Entire religions are based on coincidence.

8.

In his day, Jimmy Durante was a superstar. I suppose he could have started a small religion. I suppose any of us could start a small religion. For your next assignment, you should make a list of the people you think could start a religion and mail it to me, care of the Fourth Circle of Hell.

9.

What scares me most? The idea that my children will die before I do.

10.

What scares me least? The Afterlife. Really. Who cares? I'm going to be a good person no matter what is supposed to happen after I die.

11.

In the earthly sense, I'm terrified of heights and sudden movement. So, spiritually speaking, if one is supposed to fear God, then my God is a roller coaster. Isn't that odd?

12.

I wonder if Jimmy Durante feared roller coasters. How does Ron Padgett feel about roller coasters? I'd like to think that Dante would have understood the seductive terrors of the roller coaster.

13.

Okay, I couldn't help myself. I just asked my computer: "Was Dante's real name Durante?" And 248,000 websites collectively said, "Dante is short for Durante."

14.

Do you think, after Moses talked to the Burning Bush, that he couldn't stop himself from thinking that the bush was still burning, and presented a clear and present danger? Do you think Moses hiked back up the mountain to make sure? If I claim that, in Hebrew, Moses is spelled Mos Eisley, will you look it up? Of course, you must. Without impossible questions and unlikely answers, faith is only dust.

Sonnet, with Kobe Bean Bryant

1. My friend, X, who played D1 basketball, and was the last cut during his only NBA training camp, hasn't shot a basketball since he retired. 2. For a few years, all of his friends tried to get him to run in their pick-up games, but he refused. 3. "I hit a jumper over Shawn Kemp," he said to me. "Just one. But how could it get any better than that?" 4. What he was really saying: "Sherman, no matter how many times I score, easily and repeatedly, on you, it will never have the same magic." 5. As far as I know, he doesn't have any regrets. 6. He's a multi-sport athlete now, running ridiculous distances through the desert and swimming epic lengths in the water. And God knows what other medieval tortures he's putting himself through. 7. During his playing days, he invented a training game where he'd dribble full-court, pull up for a jumper at the top of the key, grab the rebound, make or miss, hit a lay-in, then dribble full-speed back the other way, and do the same routine on the other basket. He would do this until he vomited. Then he'd drink water, rest a few minutes, and go, go, go until he vomited again. He would do this for five or six hours at a time. 8. Have you ever done anything with such passion? 9. And here, I think of Kobe Bryant, who plays basketball with a singular ferociousness. 10. I am not a fan of the man, as a human or as a player, but I respect and fear him, in the same way that Luke Skywalker respected and feared Darth Vader. 11. Every narrative needs a villain. 12. But I suspect that Kobe loves nothing so much as he loves playing basketball. And playing it at the highest level imaginable. He is better at this one thing than all but ten or fifteen other people who have ever lived. It could be argued that he is the very best basketball player who has ever played. 13. What will he do once he is not better than everybody? When he is not the best player in the league? When he's not even the best player on his team? When he is utterly dominated by some younger and superior kid? 14. O, Kobe, when your playing days are done, I wonder if you'll also be running in the desert, not with passion, but with the fear that you'll never find where it ends.

Sonnet, with Vengeance

1. I'm a poet who spends a lot of time in Hollywood. 2. I write screenplays for movies that will never get made. 3. Through the Screenwriter's Guild, I've earned a pension that will pay me nearly $3,000 a month when I retire from writing screenplays. 4. If my writing career goes to shit, I can certainly live well on my reservation for $3,000 a month. 5. Why does an Indian work in Hollywood? Who has done Indians more harm than white filmmakers? 6. For instance: During the making of a Western, the Italian director looked at a group of Indians, pointed at one paler Sioux, and said, "Get him out of there. He's not Indian enough." 7. For instance: *Dances With Wolves*. 8. I rarely write screenplays about Indians. I have written screenplays about superheroes, smoke jumpers, pediatric surgeons, all-girl football teams, and gay soldiers. 9. I often dream of writing a B-movie about an Indian vigilante. 10. No, not a vigilante. That would be too logical. Who needs more logical violence? Who needs yet another just war? 11. Though I haven't written a word of my B-movie screenplay, I have designed the poster: An Indian man, impossibly strong and impossibly handsome, glares at us, his audience. He's bare-chested and holds a sledgehammer in one hand and a pistol in the other. The name of the movie: *Johnny Fire*. The tagline: "He's just pissed." 12. No logic. It will be the simple story of an Indian man who wakes one morning and decides to destroy everything in his life. 13. "Rage, rage, against the dying of the light." 14. When I was seven, during a New Year's Eve party at my house, I watched two Indian men fistfight on our front lawn. Then one of the Indians pulled a pistol and shot the other Indian in the stomach. As my mother rushed me back inside the house, I heard the wounded man ask, "Why does it hurt so much?"

Sonnet, with Venom

1. "Red touch yellow, kill a fellow. Red touch black, friend to Jack." 2. Yes, supposedly, you can tell the difference between deadly coral snakes and non-deadly king snakes by reciting a poem. 3. I wish it were a better poem. 4. "A narrow Fellow in the Grass/Occasionally rides— / You may have met Him—Did you not / his notice sudden is . . . " 5. That's the beginning of a great poem by Emily Dickinson. Don't you love the "is" that sounds like a hiss? 6. How many poems did Ms. Dickinson write about snakes? 6. Let's do an Internet search. 7. Couldn't find the answer. But some scholar would know. Please send the exact number to me care of this poem. 8. Another question: Did Emily Dickinson ever write a poem about the spiritual nature of snakebites? 9. I don't know one person who's been bitten by a snake. How is that possible? Why don't I know anybody who's been bitten? 10. I grew up on a reservation that is shaped like a rattlesnake. 11. Rattlesnakes swim in the ponds, creeks, and rivers where I swam. 12. At Blue Creek, on a rock face, rattlesnakes built an apartment building of burrows. I once climbed up that face. I'm lying. I'm not that brave and stupid. On a dare, my cousin climbed up that wall of burrows on a hot summer day and did not get bit. 13. My grandmother, before she died, said, "Back in the old days, Indians believed if you got bit by a rattlesnake and survived, you could spit on your enemies and poison them." 14. I once found a rattlesnake egg. I cracked it open and found a sepia photo of Emily Dickinson and my grandmother tugging on either end of a snake that was either poisonous or not.

Sonnet, without Salmon

1.The river is empty. 2. Empty of salmon, I mean. 3. But if you were talking to my grandmother, she would say the water doesn't matter if the salmon are gone. 4. She never said that. I just did. But I'm giving her those words as a gesture of love. 5. She's been gone for thirty-one years. 6. The water doesn't matter if my grandmother is gone. 7. She swam wearing all of her clothes, even her shoes. 8. I don't know if that was a tribal thing to do, or if she was just eccentric. 9. Has anybody ever said that dam building is an act of war against Indians? 10. And, yet, we need the electricity, too. 11. My mother says the reservation needs a new electrical grid because of all the brown- and blackouts. 12. "Why so many power outages?" I ask her. 13. "All the computers," she says. 14. Today, in Seattle, I watched a cute couple at the next table whispering to their cell phones instead of to each other. But, chivalrous, he walked to the self-service coffee bar to get her a cup. Lovely, I thought. She was busy on her phone while he was ten feet away. When he sat back down, she said, "Oh, I was texting you to tell you to get me sugar and cream."

Sonnet, with Slope

1. We live on a street with a 45-degree slope. 2. We live in a tall house with a twenty-seven-step staircase that changes direction twice as it rises toward our front door. 3. Therefore, we don't get trick-or-treaters. 4. Every year, we set out a big bowl of candy. But nobody ever touches it. We could use the same candy for a decade. It would be the archaeology of candy.   5. It only snows once or twice a year in our city, and freezes maybe ten times, but when it does, our street becomes the north face of a dormant volcano. 6. My wife and I pop popcorn, sit in our picture window, and watch cars slalom and careen down our hill. Again and again, we yell, "Don't hit your brakes!" 7. They always hit their brakes. 8. We once helped push a Prius out of our snow-drifted front yard. The driver, a woman in a tiny black dress, was lost on her way to a party. 9. Twenty years ago, before we moved onto the block, a driver sped down the hill and killed a little girl. 10. Every day, somebody drives dangerously fast down our street. 11. Last week, a car roared *up* our hill. 12. My neighbor and I, talking in his driveway, both yelled, "Slow down!" The white driver braked hard, furiously leapt out of his car, looking to fight, but stopped short when he saw that my neighbor and I are large, brown-skinned men. We smiled as the white man stepped back into his car and drove away. 13. A few days earlier, three blocks to the south, a black man had punched and killed a white man during a traffic dispute. 14. An eighty-foot pine, growing at an acute angle in our steep backyard, leaned like a lover toward our house. Our friend the arborist said, "Every tree, no matter where you put it, is going to fall eventually." On his advice, we cut it down.

Sonnet, With Some Things That I Have Seen

1. A red wedding dress, complete with matching train and veil, for sale in a bridal shop window. 2. A gecko chases a tarantula into a drainpipe. 3. A pine tree grows out of the split in another, larger pine tree. 4. A turtle, de-shelled by the pavement, after the man in the car speeding in front of me throws it out the window. 5. A huge, white spider, species unknown, sits on my big brother's chest as he naps on the couch. 6. The tarantula chases the gecko back out of the drainpipe. 7. On a crowded city street, a woman who, after the wind blows her skirt up and reveals that she isn't wearing underwear, laughs and bows for the sidewalk audience. 8. A man clips and eats his fingernails on a city bus. 9. A black bear sleeping on the roof of a Catholic church rolls over the edge and falls safely, still sleeping, through a car sunroof into the driver's seat. 10. A hummingbird—that somehow made its way into our refrigerator—flies out when my sister opens the door, and then confusedly hovers above the dining table just before it escapes out the window. 11. Dangerously tired as I drive home to the reservation, I am startled awake by an impossibly bright explosion that turns out to be the Northern Lights, which makes me think I'm looking directly into God's eyes. 12. A Monarch butterfly perches on the damp nose of a dog that waits patiently and silently, for at least three minutes, until that butterfly rises away. 13. My Little League son, age eight, catches a hot grounder, tags the base and a surprised runner, for the first unassisted double play of his life. 14. Am I defined by what I've seen, or do I define the world by what I've witnessed? O, what beautiful or terrible thing waits around the next corner? Who isn't in love with this mystery?

Sonnet, with Elevation

1. The pretty woman in Prada eyewear flies a C-17 for the National Guard and tests planes for Boeing. 2. I don't mean to objectify the woman by calling her pretty, but I feel okay about it because she was wearing Prada eyewear with her flight uniform. 3. And lipstick. 4. And mascara. 5. When I saw her and another pretty woman standing near the C-17, I assumed they were the pilots, and asked, "How long have you two been flying?" 6. Unlike another man on the father-and-son field trip, who asked them, "So where are the pilots?" 7. "Have you flown into combat?" I asked the women. "Yes," they said. 8. Should I have even mentioned their physical attractiveness? Well, I thought the C-17 was gorgeous, too. Aren't curves always lovelier than straight lines? Should I not mention that, either? 9. Eating MREs for lunch, I told the other fathers, "My brother and I are the first generation of men in our family who haven't served in the U.S. Military." The other men had not served, either. "Well," I added. "We're the first generation who hasn't served since my family was fighting the United States military." A couple of the other fathers seemed alarmed. Was I some kind of terrorist? "I'm Spokane Indian," I said. "Originally from the reservation. My great-great-great grandfather fought against the U.S. Cavalry. But his son fought for the U.S. in World War I." 10. The MREs these days are pretty damn good. I had beef ravioli cooked in a portable plastic bag heater. My son had spaghetti and meatballs. 11. "Always hungry," the soldier host said. "In combat, you starve." 12. The supply clerk, a Latina, had braces on her teeth. At age forty-two. "I had mine for six years," I said. We commiserated about the canker sores and ragged gums. Then she asked me, "Are you Chicano?" 13. "My parents couldn't afford to get me braces when I was a kid," she said. "So here I am, a grandmother, with bread stuck in my teeth." 14. In the control tower, I saw a helicopter zigzag toward the runway, but it just was a smudge of dirt on the window Then I saw a C-17, as regal as a blue whale, lift into the sky. Sometimes, those cargo planes carry food; sometimes they carry tanks.

Sonnet, with Snow

1. June in Northern Montana, and I was trapped on the wrong side of the Rockies by a snowstorm. 2. Trapped. By. Snow. In. June. 3. I hadn't seen my wife and sons in a week, and I missed them like lost astronauts miss oxygen, so I briefly considered wrapping chains around my tires and driving the pass anyway. 4. But what father wants to die when his sons are too young to carry the coffin? 5. So I checked into a small motel in a town I'd first assumed was more ghost than host. 6. Only twenty bucks a night! Far too cheap to be safe! 7. "There's a radiator," said the owner, an elderly white man. "But it doesn't work. Some guy painted it red, gave it to us free, and called it art." 8. In the fantastically tidy room, I slept beneath a quilt that was "sewn by twenty-three grandmothers." 9. As an Indian, it's easy to be terrified of small white towns. 10. As an Indian, it's easy to be terrified of little Indian towns. 11. But the only thing to fear was a deer. 12. A deer that, in my nightmare, smashed through the window and stood, fierce and bloody, at the foot of my bed. 13. I woke, jumped out of bed, smashed and cut my leg against that red radiator, and ran out the door into the snow. 14. When I stopped, suddenly cold, I looked back and saw my bloody footprints. I looked to my left and saw a deer, dangerously thin. And then I saw another starving deer. And another. And another. Then I looked to my right and watched that old white man reach into a paper bag, pull out an ear of corn, and throw it toward the deer. Then he threw another ear of corn. And another. And another. Such a strange tableau in the snow: man and man and deer, eager to feed, all illuminated by the stars, traveling toward and away from us at light speed.

Sonnet, with Public Address System

1. At Philadelphia International Airport, they have rocking chairs placed at strategic intervals. 2. Delayed for hours, I wanted to rock, rock, rock, and rock. 3. But the chairs were all taken so I used my carry-on as a pillow and my coat as a blanket, and fell asleep at an unused gate. 4. Twenty minutes later, a full flight arrived at the gate and disembarked. 5. Most folks ignored me, lying in the corner, but one man smiled and waved. I waved back. He hurried over to me. 6. "Oh," he said. "I thought you were somebody I went to high school with." 7. This was before Facebook, when the best social network was running into old friends and lovers in the airports. 8. "Oh, my God, I haven't seen you since you poured acid on my heart and fed it to those barn owls." 9. Among the innumerable people and ideas murdered on 9-11: Arriving and departing travelers can no longer share tearful goodbyes or ecstatic reunions at the gate. 10. Yes, it happens just outside security, but it's not the same, damn it. 11. Because the arriving fliers have had time to use the restroom, make a few phone calls, and stretch their legs on the long walk toward baggage claim. They have reclaimed the earth after hours in the sky. 12. Because the departing fliers, having checked in at least an hour before departure, and disrobed for security, must wander the airport alone. Their leave-taking is extended, even distorted. 13. And, O, here we are again in the sad-ass cell phone waiting lot: "Call me when you've reached baggage claim but before you've claimed your bags." 14. Circling the airport, I look down and see my neighborhood. I look for my house. And there it is. Somewhere between my abode and the airport, my wife and sons are driving to meet me. I've only been gone two days but I hope they break through the gate, run along the runway, and leap high enough to see me through the airplane windows.

Sonnet, with Tainted Love

1. My teenage niece, after listening to my *Motown's Greatest Hits* CD during a six-hour road trip, asked, "Why do they keep calling every woman 'Baby'?" 2. Good question. 3. In this slightly more enlightened era, what are the acceptable terms of romantic endearment that men can say to women? 4. "Baby" is way down on the list. 5. And yet, "Nobody puts Baby in the corner," from *Dirty Dancing* is one of the more romantic movie lines of my generation. 6. But I saw *Dirty Dancing* soon after a female electrical worker disappeared from a rural power station near my reservation. 7. "Signs of a struggle," read the newspaper story. 8. Nearly twenty-five years later, it's a cold case. I search for the latest news. Nobody knows what happened. Her husband and co-workers are still mourning. 9. But the husband has also remarried and had children. He says his new wife has helped him grieve and recover. 10. Good for him. Good for her. 11. The world is equal parts magic and loss. 12. I have this recurring nightmare where huge men break into our house. While defending my wife and children, I tear the invaders into pieces and eat them. 13. Jungians would suggest that I am metaphorically eating myself. 14. Even though some of us believe otherwise, men love violently.

Sonnet, with Saxophone

1. This poem doesn't contain a saxophone or any reference to music, played with or without the saxophone. 2. This poem, though written by a Native American, will not contain any reference to Native Americans or, more idiomatically speaking, Indians, or, speaking in slang, Skins. 3. This poem will not be funny. 4. This poem is very funny. 5. No, it's not. 6. I once loved a woman who played the saxophone. This was back in high school. She was a white girl, raised in a house surrounded by farmland, though her family did not farm. To get to her house, one had to drive almost a mile down a dirt road between fields of wheat. Therefore, wheat became and has remained for me the most erotic grain. 7. So, yes, this poem now contains a saxophone. And some humor. Sexy wheat? Sexy wheat! 8. *Sexy Wheat* is now the official title of this poem. 9. That white girl's father hated me because I was Indian. 10. Well, yes, I "was" Indian, but I'm Indian now, too. I've always been Indian, even when I didn't want to be. 11. While I was making love with that high school girl (don't worry, I was in high school, too), I never once paused to think, or say aloud, "I am an Indian." 12. I have the urge to call up that girl's father and tell him that I resented, but understood, his hatred of my Indian-ness, but that I never made love to his daughter *as* an Indian. 13. Although, this morning, as I brushed my teeth, I thought, "I'm an Indian brushing his teeth." But, strangely enough, as I flossed soon after brushing, I only thought, "I'm flossing my teeth." I have no explanation for this. But I'll make one up right now: It has something to do with wheat. 14. That white girl whom I loved never once played the saxophone.

Sonnet, without Stuntmen

1. Okay, if you've ever felt immortal, please raise your hand. 2. As Indian boys, we turned the reservation into a test of our immortality. 3. For instance, we climbed to the tops of pine trees, stood on the thinnest branches that threatened to snap under our weight, and leapt from one pine to another. 4. Nobody ever fell. 5. Not quite true. One kid fell, slashing against bark and cone for fifteen or twenty feet, before he grabbed a branch and saved himself. 6. The Indian Health Service doctor removed over one hundred slivers from that kid's skin. 7. For some reason, the tribe had dumped a pile of huge and unused sewer pipes down a sand hill behind the school. And we Indian boys turned it into a playground. 8. Once, I crawled to the top of a pipe, propped high into the air by other pipes, and hung off the edge by my fingertips. I was twenty feet off the ground. 9. Nothing is immortal, but some things live for a long-ass time. There's a fungal colony in Oregon that's been alive for 2,400 years. 10. Yeah, those fungi were toddlers when Jesus Christ was rambling around with his twelve buddies. 11. Here's a curse: "I don't want to live forever; I just want to live longer than you." 12. I knew an Indian who leapt from a thirty-foot cliff and dove toward a shallow pool only three feet in diameter. 13. I wasn't there when he crashed into the rocks and died. Why didn't any of the other Indians try to stop him? Because they thought he'd survive. 14. I'm not afraid of death; I'm afraid of Indians who are not afraid of death.

Sonnet, with Bird

1. Seventeen months after I moved off the reservation, and on the second plane flight of my life, I traveled to London to promote my first internationally published book. 2. A Native American in England! I imagined the last Indian in England was Maria Tall Chief, the Osage ballerina who was once married to Balanchine. An Indian married to Balanchine! 3. My publishers put me in a quaint little hotel near the Tate Gallery. I didn't go into the Tate. Back then, I was afraid of paintings of and by white men. I think I'm still afraid of paintings of and by white men. 4. This was long before I had a cell phone, so I stopped at payphones to call my wife. I miss the intensity of a conversation measured by a dwindling stack of quarters. 5. No quarters in England, though, and I don't remember what the equivalent British coin was called. 6. As with every other country I've visited, nobody thought I was Indian. This made me lonely. 7. Lonely enough to cry in my hotel bed one night as I kept thinking, "I am the only Indian in this country right now. I'm the only Indian within a five-thousand-mile circle." 8. But I wasn't the only Indian; I wasn't even the only Spokane Indian. 9. On the payphone, my mother told me that a childhood friend from the reservation was working at a London pub. So I wrote down the address and took a taxi driven by one of those cabdrivers with extrasensory memory. 10. When I entered the pub, I sat in a corner, and waited for my friend to discover me. When he saw me, he leapt over the bar and hugged me. "I thought I was the only Indian in England," he said. 11. His name was Aaron and he died of cancer last spring. I'd rushed to see him in his last moments, but he passed before I could reach him. Only minutes gone, his skin was still warm. I held his hand, kissed his forehead, and said, "England." 12. "England," in our tribal language, now means, "Aren't we a miracle?" and "Goodbye." 13. In my strange little hotel near the Tate, I had to wear my suit coat to eat breakfast in the lobby restaurant. Every morning, I ordered eggs and toast. Everywhere in the world, bread is bread, but my eggs were impossibly small. "What bird is this?" I asked the waiter. "That would be quail," he said. On the first morning, I could not eat the quail eggs. On the second morning, I only took a taste. On third day, I ate two and ordered two more. 14. A gathering of quail is called a bevy. A gathering of Indians is called a tribe. When quails speak, they call it a song. When Indians sing, the air is heavy with grief. When quails grieve, they lie down next to their dead. When Indians die, the quail speaks.

One More Sonnet for My Father, Who Died in March 2003, Though I Sometimes Misremember and Think That He Died in 2004

Mr. Grief,
Dr. Grief,
Mrs. Grief,
Miss Grief,
Herr Grief,
Sir Grief,
Lady Grief,
Duke Grief,

Fuck
You,
Fuck
You, You
Memory
Thief.

III Odes to Now

Loud Ghazal

Who among you thinks that I am afraid of silence
Because I can't find your version of God with silence?

I hear God in a pinball machine's sound and fury.
You say you can't? Are your ears clogged with silence?

I hear angel wings in a bowling ball's low rumble.
You can't? Have you been struck odd with silence?

God is a siren screaming toward a house on fire.
Lives will be saved by water cannons, not with silence.

God is the raucous laughter during and after sex.
Make noise! Joyful noise! Don't fallow sod with silence.

Have you ever heard great powwow drummers singing to God?
Pay them! Pay them! Gas can't be bought with silence.

When I start my car I hear a dinosaur's grief song.
To live, we kill. Don't be so distraught with silence.

God is a knife that slices root and neck for food.
Make joyful noise! Don't dishonor blood with silence.

I hear God when my son plays his alto saxophone.
Am I strange? Or have you been struck odd with silence?

I hear God whenever I hear my neighbors make love.
You can't? Maybe your ears are clogged with silence.

Have you ever heard one thousand cranes lift into flight?
It sounds like a hymn. Don't confuse God with silence.

Faith should be quarrel and quandary.
Why not make noise? Why haven't you fought with silence?

Ode to Now

If I celebrate our time in our time,
      Then I will be mocked
        And maligned,
    But I still choose to love the clock's
Forward momentum. I praise grind and climb.
I praise the arriving minutes and hours,
      However beautiful, cruel, dumb,
        Or dour.

Today, I praise "Alison" by Elvis Costello, instead of praising *Politics* by Aristotle. I praise Elvis Costello's chorus: "Alison, I know this world is killing you. Oh, Alison, my aim is true." Don't you wish your lover, as you intertwine naked in bed, would say such a thing to you? Isn't that the kind of dialogue—the spoken promise and pledge—that we want from our lovers? Wouldn't you tremble if your lover, if any of your potential lovers, said to you, "O, the world is a cruel and dishonest place; human beings are cruel and dishonest; but I, a human being, will be the one who proves otherwise." When it comes to love, yes, we want to kiss mouths and lick thighs, but aren't we truly searching for the otherwise? When it comes to love, yes, we trade excuses and lies, but aren't we truly searching for the otherwise? Say it! Sing it! "O, my lover, please, be otherwise. O, my lover, please, be otherwise." But, damn, don't our lovers always disappoint us? And don't we always disappoint our lovers? Just listen to Elvis Costello's sadness: "But I heard you let that little friend of mine take off your party dress." How does one ever recover from such painful shit? And yet, we do recover. With seismic hearts, we build and rebuild cities. With seismic hearts, we build and rebuild countries. With seismic hearts, we send probes into the lonely expanse of space, in the hopes of finding some other forms of life, and all of those probes are playing sad rock songs, because we know, we know, we know that seismic hearts are universal. And yes, those probes also carry the wise words of Aristotle, but you can't dance to Aristotle. You can't wrap your arms around your lover's shoulders or hips and shuffle along to Aristotle. Aristotle is about reason. Aristotle is about finite structure. Aristotle is about conclusion. But we human beings, and our music, we are unreasonable, destructive, and relentless. And so, if I celebrate our unreasonable, destructive, and relentless souls, then I will likely be viewed as a cruel and limited boy.

If I celebrate our time in our time,
        Then I will likely be accused
           Of some crime
      Or another, but I still choose
To praise the present. And if you find
That disagreeable, then kiss my ass—
       The only part of me always
          Looking back.

Ode to "My Sharona"

It opens with that insistent drumbeat—
      And then comes that filthy bass riff—
      And then he pleads—
    He sings—he preaches—he lifts—
He st-st-st-st-st-stammers his need
For Sharona. He doesn't hedge or hide—
    He interrogates—he declares—
      He sweats and swears—
He loves her kind—he wants her eyes and thighs—

And, damn, it makes me remember how much
    I wanted to solve the mystery—
      To ask and touch
    That girl—that girl—that pretty,
Pretty girl—O, hush—O, rush—O, blush—
She was every other constellation—
    She was a powwow bonfire—
      A red choir—
A deer drum shaking the reservation—

And though I haven't kissed her in decades,
    I can still feel the sweet hurt
    Of removing her shirt—
Jesus, her scent and taste refuse to fade—
She was heat lightning—she was corona—
    She was storm—she was river flood—
    She was the salt inside my blood—
She was—she was—she was my Sharona.

Ode to "Jolene"

There is no lyric more painful than this:
        "He talks about you in his sleep."
            That's tragic shit.
        Dolly Parton's song roars with need
And envy. It's a fist—no, it's a kick
To the crotch. Can you imagine how it feels
        To beg a romantic rival
            To not steal
        Your lover? Have you been defiled
Like that? Have you ever been that peeled

And husked? Have you ever been that exposed?
        How do any of us find the strength
            To remove our clothes
        And give away the width, depth, and breadth
Of our fragile bodies and finite souls
When we can be so easily replaced
        By a new lover? By the next
            Prettier face?
        By the one who offers better sex?
By the one who fucks with more or less grace?

Dear God, it hurts to listen to this song.
        It makes one fall to one's knees
        In fear of infidelity:
Don't do it. Don't do it. Don't do me wrong.
Dear God, this song is more like a death scream:
        There is a pale daughter
        Riding in for the slaughter,
And her name is Jolene, Jolene, Jolene, Jolene.

She is the fire that burns between us.
She is the redheaded, green-eyed witch
Who preaches and teaches us this:
Dolly Parton is a heartbreaking genius.

Dear God, thank you for Dolly's white blues—
For music that stays unafraid
To lament the relentless ways
In which we lose and lose and lose and lose.

Another Proposition

1. Protogyny

Each male sheephead fish keeps a harem
Of females. But when that dude succumbs,
The harem's dominant female becomes

A male. Yes, this fish changes gender
To propagate. How bizarre and tender.
Did God create the world with a blender?

Who cares? Let's just celebrate the splendor.

2. Protandry

If two clownfish males meet and decide
To mate, the dominant one will cast aside
Boyish things and become female. Why

Would God create a transsexual fish?
Well, speaking as an evolutionist,
I think it's because death is relentless

And we must breed creatively or we'll vanish.

3. Protean

Kangaroos do auto-fellatio.
Gay male penguins will nest and use stones
As surrogate eggs. Fire ants, komodo

Dragons, and sharks have given virgin birth.
If one believes that God created the Earth,
Then one should believe God creates with mirth,

Because the world is delightfully perverse.

4. Pro and Con

"But, Sherman," he said, "Gay marriage is unnatural. If we let gay people get married, then we might as well let people marry dogs. Or fish. Homosexuality is an abomination. Homosexuality is a sin. Sherman, gay men threaten the institution of marriage. Gay men threaten your marriage."

"Actually," I said, "Gay men catered my marriage. You want to know who really threatens my marriage? Who threatens any straight man's marriage? Beautiful straight women with no boundaries."

Alphabet

Z
Bone broken in two
Places by a lightning bolt.

Y
Americans see a goalpost
After the Apocalypse.
Non-Americans see a tree heavy with fruit
That Americans won't eat.

X
If you can't build a fire
By nightfall,
You will die from the cold.

W
Naked, I press my ear to her chest
And count the hours.

V
Filter, who do you love more:
The coffee grounds
Or the boiling water?

U
Dear scientists,
Thank you
For the antibiotics.

T
Candle falling,
Will I reflexively catch you
And burn my hand?

S
Did the snake offer
The apple
Or did the apple offer
The snake?

R
Broken bee, I will keep
Your stinger
As a souvenir.

Q
Dear man-with-knife-in-head,
It's amazing that you can still talk,
But all you keep saying is,
 "Do I have a knife in my head?"

P
The little country
In the palm of my hand
Raises its flag
Of surrender.

O
Lost by a swimmer upstream,
The inner tube
Pauses to be admired.

N
Sweetheart, this is
What you sound like
When you sleep standing up.

M
Broken bridge—
My youth is
On the other side.

L
That skinny boy
With big feet is my
Lovely, lovely, lovely son.

K
Jesus, the world is
A crowded place.
An angel just elbowed
Me in the face.

J
What kind of fool
Brings an umbrella
To a gunfight?

I
Did you know
An airplane's exterior walls
Are thinner
Than its interior walls?

H
A ladder with one rung
Is a shitty ladder.

G
Dear bird, breaking
Out of the shell, I admire
Your will to live.

F
Indian woman
With hair so thick
She snapped teeth
Off the comb.

E
For years, the kitchen table's three legs
Have been looking for the fourth.

D
In bed with my wife,
We watch the window steal
Half of the moon.

C
My father never broke
His chains. Did yours?

B
Ah, I miss my wife's pregnant body.

A
Damn it, I told you
That ladder
Would collapse.

Phone Calls from Ex-Lovers

I have had very few lovers
For a man of my generation,
Tribe, and reservation.

I am revealing this, not
To make any point about sex,
Promiscuity, monogamy, or my reservation,

But to give you the information
You need in order to believe me
When I say this:

I have, in my entire life, received
Only one phone call from an ex-lover,
And that was in 1988, twenty-five years ago.

Of course, you want to know the details
Of that phone call, and, of course, I am
Going to reveal the details of that phone call

Because I am a poet, or more accurately
Stated, a metaphor-addicted gossip—
A fact that may or may not explain

My relative chastity. But in any case,
I was in college at Washington State University,
Which, in January, any January, might be

The least romantic place in the world
(Choked as it is with muddy snow seasoned
With the thin corpses of orphaned wheat).

So let me say that I was doing homework
In my studio apartment that overlooked
A coal plant (my father also smoked cigars

In my childhood home, so just imagine
That my lungs are anything but pink)
When the phone rang and I answered

Because, well, a ringing phone is
Usually answered. This is not a plot point.
This is how the world works.

So I answered the phone, mildly surprised
Because that phone rarely rang
(I was a recent transfer student

And only knew a few people).
I answered the phone and heard
The familiar voice of my ex-girlfriend.

"Hello," she said. "I got your number from your mother. She said to say hello. And I know we haven't talked in a while. But I just got back from my first date with this guy—he's a cashier/manager at the grocery store—the one we used to shop together, if you remember, and I didn't mean to, but I had sex with him in his apartment. And he was better than you in bed—well, no, he was better at one thing but not at the other thing. But why am I passing judgment on your sexual dexterity? It's beside the point. So let me get to the reason I am calling, and here it is: I hoped that having sex with somebody new would make me feel better, but it didn't. It just made me lonely, incredibly lonely, and so I called you because I miss you. But no, don't worry, I don't miss our romantic life, not at all, because you are, as you know, utterly impossible to love because you are a Democrat. But you are the best talker I know, man or woman. You are the one person I could always talk to about anything, and every conversation was important to you, including the ones that weren't important at all, and I just don't have any friends who love to talk, and to listen to me like you do, and I know you're with that other girl now, and I don't want to interfere with that, but I was hoping you would understand, and she would, too, that I just want permission to call you every once in a while, maybe once a month, or maybe once a week if things get bad, and just talk, just talk, just talk."

Now, okay, I swear this is the most accurate
Paraphrase of her phone call—her monologue—
That I can render. It's my best truth.

So I am asking you what you would do
In such a situation. Okay, well, I guess
I am just pausing here in this poem

As a narrative strategy, to create
A little tension, some drama.
In the absence of rhyme, I'm using time

As a formal device, so okay, here
Is what I did: I got off the phone
With the ex-girlfriend and called

My then-current girlfriend and told her
She had to come to my apartment
So the three of us—the ex, the current, and I—

Could discuss the ways in which
This "just talking with the ex" thing
Might work. And, believe it or not,

My current girlfriend rushed to my place
For this phone call. Now, you should know
That my current, my ex, and I all went

To the same high school and had known
One another for years. My two loves
Had even played basketball together.

My ex was a great shooter from the wing,
And my current was a quick point guard
So they had, over the years, often run

An out of bounds play their coach
Drew up on his little chalkboard:
My current girlfriend threw the out-

Of-bounds pass to my ex,
Who would drive all the way
To the hoop or take a jump shot.

You see, my ex and my current weren't friends,
But they had been teammates.
So, given these biographical details,

You will probably understand why
My current girlfriend, upon hearing
Of my ex-girlfriend's loneliness,

Simply asked, "Do you think she's okay?"
And then, upon speaking with the ex,
Consented to this "just talking" plan.

Now, looking back, I realize
That my then-current girlfriend
Was likely being my co-dependent

(It would be three more years
Before I got sober). Or it could be
That everybody in the world is more

Kind than I am and I haven't bothered
To take note of that. Or it could be—
Well, frankly, I don't what it was.

But I do know this: After making
The "just talking" agreement, my ex
Never called me again. I have not

Talked to her in twenty-five years.
Isn't it strange to think
That I saw her naked a hundred times

But will never see her in any form
Ever again? Why is it so easy
To let go of people? Of course, since

I am writing this poem, it should be
Apparent that I am not a person
Who lets go of other people.

But, anyway, as we're nearing the end
Of this poem, I am supposed to
Conclude it, to give you its theme,

But first, let me give you a little more information: I've heard gossip that my
lonely ex married a good man who sells cars and helps her raise beautiful babies.
And my then-current girlfriend left me in 1991. (Or did I leave her? Wait,
yes, I left her. Or did she leave me? Did we leave each other simultaneously?)
She eventually met a blue-collar worker, another good guy, I hear, who helps
her raise another set of beautiful babies. I haven't heard her voice in seventeen
years, though she emails me congratulations whenever I publish a new book.

And I, as you may know, have met
And married a force of nature—a woman
Who can become the weather—

And I love her like a lost man
Loves finding a GPS machine and a sack
Full of batteries in the desert,

And we are raising beautiful babies.
So, obviously, no matter what happens
Inside any particular broken romance,

Most of us, nearly all of us, just
Move on, move on, move on, move on.
And yet, there is still something more

To say about this, and so I irritably
Reach for that thing, and I want you
To remember it, to encode it

In your primate DNA, and in order
For that to happen, my final message
Needs to rhyme. Yes, I'm sorry, but

Free verse isn't designed to be
Memorized. I mean, Jesus, if you want
Proof, just turn on the radio, tune

To a classic rock station, and sing
Along with every song you know.
Count those songs. Count the lyrics,

Count the number of choruses—rhymed,
Of course—that you have memorized
Without even trying. If you're a typical

American, you'll discover that you know
The lyrics to thousands of songs
And you know those songs so well

Because they have, say it, rhythm
And rhyme. Hell, memory itself
Works in rhythm and rhyme.

To prove my point, I offer here a list of "The Top 100 Songs of 1984," the year
I lost my virginity. As you read this list, I guarantee that all of you, between
the ages of 35 and 50, will have one specific memory associated with 93% of
these songs:

1. "When Doves Cry" . . . Prince
2. "What's Love Got to Do with It" . . . Tina Turner
3. "Jump" . . . Van Halen
4. "Karma Chameleon" . . . Culture Club
5. "Like a Virgin" . . . Madonna
6. "Hello" . . . Lionel Richie
7. "Owner of a Lonely Heart" . . . Yes
8. "Against All Odds" . . . Phil Collins
9. "Footloose" . . . Kenny Loggins
10. "Ghostbusters" . . . Ray Parker, Jr.
11. "I Just Called" . . . Stevie Wonder
12. "Out of Touch" . . . Daryl Hall & John Oates
13. "Say Say Say" . . . Paul McCartney & Michael Jackson

14. "I Feel for You" . . . Chaka Khan
15. "Missing You" . . . John Waite
16. "Let's Hear It for the Boy" . . . Deniece Williams
17. "Time After Time" . . . Cyndi Lauper
18. "The Reflex" . . . Duran Duran
19. "Dancing in the Dark" . . . Bruce Springsteen
20. "Caribbean Queen" . . . Billy Ocean
21. "Talking in Your Sleep" . . . The Romantics
22. "Hard Habit to Break" . . . Chicago
23. "Let's Go Crazy" . . . Prince & The Revolution
24. "Self Control" . . . Laura Branigan
25. "The Wild Boys" . . . Duran Duran
26. "Hold Me Now" . . . Thompson Twins
27. "Jump (For My Love)" . . . Pointer Sisters
28. "Joanna" . . . Kool & The Gang
29. "Break My Stride" . . . Matthew Wilder
30. "The Glamorous Life" . . . Sheila E
31. "Somebody's Watching Me" . . . Rockwell
32. "Running with the Night" . . . Lionel Richie
33. "Penny Lover" . . . Lionel Richie
34. "That's All!" . . . Genesis
35. "Stuck on You" . . . Lionel Richie
36. "She Bop" . . . Cyndi Lauper
37. "Oh Sherrie" . . . Steve Perry
38. "99 Luftballons" . . . Nena
39. "Drive" . . . The Cars
40. "Here Comes the Rain Again" . . . Eurythmics
41. "That's Why They Call It the Blues" . . . Elton John
42. "Twist of Fate" . . . Olivia Newton-John
43. "The Heart of Rock & Roll" . . . Huey Lewis & The News
44. "Automatic" . . . Pointer Sisters
45. "Girls Just Want to Have Fun" . . . Cyndi Lauper
46. "No More Lonely Nights" . . . Paul McCartney
47. "Infatuation" . . . Rod Stewart
48. "Better Be Good to Me" . . . Tina Turner
49. "Sunglasses at Night" . . . Corey Hart
50. "I Can Dream About You" . . . Dan Hartman
51. "Sister Christian" . . . Night Ranger

52. "Borderline" . . . Madonna

53. "Purple Rain" . . . Prince & The Revolution

54. "Eyes Without a Face" . . . Billy Idol

55. "State of Shock" . . . The Jacksons

56. "The Warrior" . . . Scandal w/ Patty Smyth

57. "All Through the Night" . . . Cyndi Lauper

58. "I Want a New Drug" . . . Huey Lewis & the News

59. "If This Is It" . . . Huey Lewis & the News

60. "Miss Me Blind" . . . Culture Club

61. "Sad Songs (Say So Much)" . . . Elton John

62. "Lucky Star" . . . Madonna

63. "Almost Paradise" . . . Mike Reno & Ann Wilson

64. "Cover Me" . . . Bruce Springsteen

65. "Legs" . . . ZZ Top

66. "Strut" . . . Sheena Easton

67. "If Ever You're in My Arms Again" . . . Peabo Bryson

68. "I Can't Hold Back" . . . Survivor

69. "To All the Girls" . . . Iglesias & Nelson

70. "Love Somebody" . . . Rick Springfield

71. "You Might Think" . . . The Cars

72. "Adult Education" . . . Daryl Hall & John Oates

73. "Breakdance" . . . Irene Cara

74. "They Don't Know" . . . Tracey Ullman

75. "I'm So Excited" . . . Pointer Sisters

76. "Got a Hold on Me" . . . Christine McVie

77. "Pink Houses" . . . John Cougar Mellencamp

78. "Thriller" . . . Michael Jackson

79. "Nobody Told Me" . . . John Lennon

80. "Let the Music Play" . . . Shannon

81. "Wrapped Around Your Finger" . . . The Police

82. "Head Over Heels" . . . The Go-Go's

83. "Cruel Summer" . . . Bananarama

84. "Think of Laura" . . . Christopher Cross

85. "Magic" . . . The Cars

86. "Breakin' " . . . Ollie & Jerry

87. "New Moon on Monday" . . . Duran Duran

88. "Lights Out" . . . Peter Wolf

89. "Round and Round" . . . Ratt

90. "The Longest Time" . . . Billy Joel
91. "The Language of Love" . . . Dan Fogelberg
92. "Can't Get Over Loving You" . . . Ray Parker, Jr.
93. "Dancing in the Streets" . . . Shalamar
94. "Dark Side" . . . John Cafferty & The Beaver Brown Band
95. "Read 'Em and Weep" . . . Barry Manilow
96. "Blue Jean" . . . David Bowie
97. "Desert Moon" . . . Dennis DeYoung
98. "Doctor! Doctor!" . . . Thompson Twins
99. "An Innocent Man" . . . Billy Joel
100. "Some Guys Have All the Luck" . . . Rod Stewart

As you read the above list, I guarantee that you remembered the music and lyrics of 89% of the songs. I guarantee that if you heard any of these songs on the radio, you would be able to sing them, word for word. Why do we remember these songs, some of them obscure, so well? Because, like I said, memory itself works with rhythm and rhyme. Memory requires rhythm and rhyme. So, now, all of you, who must love poems because, well, you are

Currently reading a poem, I want you to,
Off the top of your head,
Recite lines of poetry. Free verse poetry.

I'll give you a hundred dollars
If you can quote me one hundred free verse
Poetry lines in the next one hundred minutes

Don't get me wrong. I read, write, and love
All kinds of poetry. I have a crush
On the free verse poem you are reading.

And I'm sure quite a few of you
Will fondly recall a paraphrase
Of my love-like-a-GPS-machine metaphor.

But I doubt any of you will ever be able
To accurately quote from this poem
Unless I give you a rhyming and rhythmic summation

That desperately strives to equal Springsteen,
Stevie Wonder, or Carole King.
So, here it comes, get ready, here's

My final statement on the subject
Of phone calls from ex-lovers.
Here is the concluding stanza:

There is nothing we want more
Than to remain wanted
By the ones who wanted us before.

Ode to Coffee, As Imagined by Wikipedia

In the coffee shop, the dreadlocked white dude
        Orders a complicated drink.
        "Man, don't be rude
        To that sacred liquid," I think
As the barista pours soy into the brew—
A blasphemous act—and then adds nutmeg.
        But worse, this place has the nerve
           To grind and serve
Decaffeinated coffee. God, I beg

You, please, strike me down if I ever dare
        To order that watery swill.
        There is no there *there.*
        What fool wants to go unfulfilled?
Why does this dude wear such rebellious hair,
But drink a coffee so neutered and caged?
        I want my java hot, complex,
           And, O, French-pressed.
I want my coffee to taste like sex and rage.

I want my coffee to taste like the brew
        Made from the first coffee tree
        Shipped, in the 1720s,
Into our country. That beleaguered crew
Repelled pirates, but not before they ripped
        A branch off that coffee tree.
        It was a grievous injury,
But that tree, nursed and fed, survived the trip,
And was replanted and safely reborn
        Inside a hedge of nettles and spears
        That bloodied all who came near.
Lord, I'd love my coffee to taste of those thorns.

Rest Stop

I pull off the freeway at 3 a.m.
To urinate. It feels good to go
In a dark nowhere, but then I realize,
As my night vision comes into focus,

That I am pissing in the front yard
Of a small church. Is this blasphemy?
I'm sure it is. But worse, I notice
The church is next to a gas station.

And there is a small house behind me,
A playground to the left, and a grocery
Store to my right. This is a little town
And I'm pissing in the middle of it.

But I can't stop. I can only hope
Everybody is asleep. I don't mean
To insult this small town. I love
Small towns. I was raised in small towns.

Sleep, small town folks, please sleep.
But then I realize there is a large deer
Standing on the front porch of the church.
And another deer standing beneath a broken

Beer light on the gas station. And another
Deer on the stoop of the house. And three
Or four deer on the playground. And five
Or six more on the road near my car. *Wow.*

I wonder if this is somehow a town populated
Entirely by deer. What if these deer built
The church and worship a deer, slaughtered
By hunters, but who rose from the dead?

What if these deer built that gas station
But fill the tanks with bark and seed? What
If these deer built that house and sleep
In beds made of tree stumps and wild grass?

What if these deer built that playground
And swing from the bars by their antlers?
The deer, suddenly as bright and silent
As the stars, stare at me. They can smell me,

My human stink, my piss, my predator breath.
I am a dangerous stranger, but then, pop,
A porch light snaps on, a front door opens,
And a large human—a male—steps out

Of the house. The deer startle and run.
I zip up my pants and run with them.
I can't keep up, of course. There's no way
Any human can keep pace with a deer,

But then suddenly, I do. I run beside
A deer that looks at me with such comic
Surprise that I laugh and nearly fall,
But no, I run and run and run and run.

We race through the thick woods. We leap
Fallen trees and brush. We bunch together
To form a knot then we break apart
And splash separate paths through a creek.

We climb a rise to the top of the ridge
And just when I wonder if we'll fly, we don't.
We crest and run with terrifying speed down
The steep slope. O, I hope, I hope I don't fall,

And then I do fall. If one hopes not to fall
Then one will surely fall, and so I do fall,
Falling and rolling down the hill, as the deer
Leave me behind, as I thud to a stop against

The base of a tree, as I stare up through
The branches to see the night sky, the stars,
The new constellation of one sad and lonely man
Chasing and failing to catch a herd of deer.

Crow Justice

As I pump gas, a flock of crows passes
Overhead. Then another flock arrives,
And another, and a third, fourth, and fifth.
Jesus, the sky itself is made of crows,
And they're louder than the nearby freeway.
Could this be a family reunion?
Maybe these dark birds are planning for war.
Then, with one great hush, the flock goes silent,
And separates into living currents,
And forms winged rivers around a mid-air
Island of three quickly deserted crows.
Why? I don't know at first, but then one bird,
Much larger than the rest, breaks from the flock,
Quickly followed by other large, fast birds,
And leads a mass attack on the lost crows
And *snap-snap-snaps* their necks, and as they fall,
Tears them in half. As the crow-pieces hit
Hot pavement, the flock, as one, celebrates.
Yes, they celebrate. And I realize
That I saw a public execution.
A murder of crows, indeed, but what crimes,
Among the crows, are punishable by
Death? I can't begin to understand crow
Morality. Hey, I don't want to try,
But justice, like time, flies and flies and flies.

Aware, Unaware

Be quick now and pull to the roadside
Because bad drivers don't know they're bad drivers,
And the architects of genocide
Always think of themselves as survivors.

New York, Interrupted

Ascending
From
Subway
To
Street,
I'm
Always
Confused—

I don't live in New York. I use the subway when I visit, so I keep a stack of partially used MetroCards on my desk in Seattle. When I first traveled to New York, I used subway tokens. They are useless now, but I still keep a dish filled with those eccentric coins. Today, I counted my MetroCards. There are fifty-three. For years, I've tried to remember to bring them when I travel to NYC. But what's the use? I will always forget. So what should I do with these cards? Maybe I'll mail one each to fifty-three friends who live in NYC. I'll write them a note: "I love you, dear friend. I love you inside and in between the boroughs. These MetroCards are a mystery. Use them. Unmask them. Interrogate them. Be thorough." Or maybe I should send all fifty-three to the visiting poet who met her future husband on the F Train. "Really?" New Yorkers (surprised by their city) ask when I repeat that story. "Yes," I say. "She met him on the subway when she asked him for directions." Is that a miracle? Maybe. But, hell, I know a guy—a lifelong New Yorker—who lost his virginity as he was crossing the Brooklyn Bridge. Is that a miracle? He says, "Fucking A, it was a miracle, all thirty-three seconds of it."

—Descending
From
Street
To
Subway,
I'm
Always
Confused.

Jesus at the Bethlehem B&B

I didn't rise from the tomb
To share a goddamn bathroom.

License to Kill

Lu Wu wrote:
  "The rat steals rice only if
  The moon allows it to happen."

*

Aristotle Polatkin wrote:
  "A good man would share his potato
  With the rat. But I am starving,
  And a starving man is never a good man."

*

Red Dog wrote:
  "We gave the white man the land and the sky,
  And he gave us a rifle loaded with rats."

*

As the handyman fixed our crawlspace door, I complained about the rats that had invaded the place and were living in the insulation.

"Well, all that snow and ice drove a bunch of rats indoors," he said. "The rats like to come in from the cold."

I laughed, thinking of that James Bond movie, *The Spy Who Came In from the Cold.* So, to show off for the handyman, I remembered and renamed all of the other Bond thrillers:

Dr. Rat
From Russia with Rat
Ratfinger
Thunderrat
You Only Live Rat
Rat Royale
On Her Rat's Secret Service
Rats Are Forever

LiveRat and Let Rat
The Rat with the Golden Gun
The Rat Who Loved Me
Moonrat
For Your Rat Only
Ratpussy
Never Say Rat Again
A View to a Rat
The Living Ratlights
License to Rat
GoldenRat
Tomorrow Never Rats
The Rat is Not Enough
Rat Another Day
Casino Rat
Quantum of Rat

"Wow," the handyman said. "That's a lot of movies."

"Yeah," I said. "I even remembered the Lazenby Bond movie, and one with Peter Sellers and David Niven, though I don't remember which one played Bond. Probably David Niven. Woody Allen has a cameo in that one."

"You've always had a good memory like that?" the handyman asked.

"Yeah, pretty much."

"Must have really helped you in college and stuff, I guess."

"Yeah, I guess."

The handyman went back to his work. He lifted the metal door onto the hinges.

"Yeah," he said. "This steel door will be a lot better than that cardboard one that was in here. Rats won't be able to chew through this sucker."

"Cool," I said. "Thank you so much."

"No worries," he said. "But there's something else."

"What?"

"That movie, the one that got you joking, *The Spy Who Came In from the Cold*, it's not a Bond movie."

"Yes, it is."

"No, that one stars Richard Burton. He's a British spy in it, but he ain't playing James Bond."

I thought about it for a bit. And remembered.

"Yeah," I said. "You're right. That one is about the Cold War."
The handyman smiled.
"Our side won the Cold War, didn't we?" he asked.
"I think so," I said. "But I'm not sure I trust my memory anymore."
"That's okay," he said. "The rats must have distracted you."

*

Xiao Yi wrote:
    "The flower remembers nothing
    Except the honeybee."

*

Ariana X. Rodriguez wrote:
    "There is a word in Nahuatl that means:
    "All of the memory in the world."
    Nobody remembers how to say the word.

*

Einstein wrote:
    "The Universe is constructed of memory.
    Unless it's not."

Bestiary

1.

My mother sends me a black-and-white photograph of her and my father,
    circa 1968, posing with two Indian men.

"Who are those Indian guys?" I ask her on the phone.

"I don't know," she says.

The next obvious question: "Then why did you send me this photo?"
    But I don't ask it.

One of those strange Indian men is pointing up toward the sky.

Above them, a bird shaped like a question mark.

2.

My mother is a quilter. She makes five hundred dollars for each.

My father, drunk, during a horseshoe game in 1976, hit fourteen
    ringers in a row.

My neighbors owned a horse that thought it was a dog. It ran with
    the neighborhood pack and lifted a back leg to pee against trees.

That horse also equine-howled at the moon.

So maybe that horse thought it was a wolf, since all of the dogs
    remembered they once were wolves.

My mother made a star quilt for that horse. And it would walk in circles,
    tamping imaginary grass, before it lay down on my mother's gift.

3.

I pulled the trigger once,

Twice,

Thrice,

And a fourth

And fifth time,

But purposely missed each because I didn't want to kill the aluminum
can perched on the junkyard refrigerator. And I didn't want to
disappoint my father, who had never shot at any animal, but still
owned eleven hunting rifles.

4.

The monsters that live on my reservation:

A car-sized snapping turtle that lives in, of course, Turtle Lake, and
only appears when great sins are committed.

A bear, on fire, that rumbles through the woods around Benjamin Lake.

An insect that lands on your chest and sucks oxygen from your lungs.

A deer with smaller deer growing out of each antler point.

Spiders that hunt in packs.

5.

Have you seen a photo of the mouse with a human ear growing out
of its back?

Have you ever, when speaking to your wife, answered a question
she didn't ask?

I told the high school class: "If we ever get trapped in the mountains,
like the Donner Party, I'll have no trouble eating any of you."

They laughed. They thought I was kidding.

My answer: "Sometimes, I feel like taking off my clothes and running,
on fire, through the woods." Her question: "Have you seen
Joe's saxophone?"

What do you think that mouse hears?

6.

The famous writer, in Paris, leads me through a maze of streets to a small
plot of grass surrounded closely by apartment buildings, and says,
"This is where I had sex with Catherine Deneuve."

I've been to Paris three times since then and cannot find that place.

I feel like an eleven-year-old when I say this: Everything in the world is
made of sex.

Has there ever been an animal on earth more beautiful than
Catherine Deneuve, circa 1968?

I'd vote for my mother, circa 1968, if it didn't sound creepy.

Above all of us, birds shaped like question marks.

Possible Epitaphs for My Gravestone

After Ernest Hilbert

I ate too much meat, or so you allege,
But now the earthworms are getting revenge.

Why did you bury me with a hand drum?
This whole Indian thing is overdone.

Is this death? Is this death? Is this death? Is this death?
If life is a marathon, then I'm out of breath.

What is my legacy?
I wrote some poetry.

This is the first time that I've taken repose.
If you can read this, then you're standing too close.

I end where I began:
I've lost my keys again.

An Indian's life is a series of losses,
But at least I died of natural causes.

IV   My Indian Names

Monosonnet for Grief, Interrupted

My
Friend
Boo
Says
He
Fights
His
Sadness

(As a toddler, I loved to rub my face against my big sister's pantyhosed leg. This was in 1967, and my sister would soon leave our reservation to join the ecstatic masses in San Francisco. There, she rolled down her pantyhose and had sex with dozens of men, got pregnant, and came back home to give birth to my niece. Always chaotic, my big sister gave up custody of her baby to our aunt and then shacked up with a series of white men before she married an Indian guy named Steve, moved to Montana, and died in a drunken house fire when I was fourteen. Whenever I think of her death, I remember Gerard Manley Hopkins' poem, "No worst, there is none. Pitched past pitch of grief/ More pangs will, schooled at forepangs, wilder wring. / Comforter, where, where is your comforting?/ Mary, mother of us, where is your relief?" My sister's name was Mary. Her daughter—my niece—often asks me about her, but I barely knew her. I just remember that, despite her continual sadness, she always seemed to be joyous. I just remember that, in my high school years, when the girls still wore pantyhose and let me roll them down only a little past their knees, I was equal parts joy and grief.)

By
Drinking
Large
Glasses
Of
Water

Roll, Baby, Roll

Jesus, could it be the DJ played
    "Love to Love You, Baby,"
        Donna Summer's seventeen-minute orgasm,
For the teenagers skating
    At Pattison's North Roller Rink
        In Spokane, Washington?

This was in '77 or '78,
    When the good people of Spokane
        Were busy burning books and records—
When talk radio was afire
    With warnings about rock star demons
        And their disco orgies—

So it couldn't be true
    That Donna Summer's seventeen-minute orgasm
        Was the last song of the night—
The last couples' dance.
    But I remember it that way.
        I remember my pretty cousin

Rolling a slow and romantic circle
    With some skinny white boy—
        A Hillyard neighborhood hippie—
Who wrapped one arm around my cousin's waist
    And waved his other hand
        Along with the music

Like a white trash ballet boy
    Or a trailer park maestro.
        I was an unbalanced kid,
Barely able to skate solo,
    So I leaned against a railing
        And watched my cousin skate

With her temporary boyfriend,
Who had more grace at sixteen
Than he would ever have again.
Jesus, I was jealous.
I instantly hated that white boy
And I wanted to punch him

In the head as he ran his hand
Up and down my cousin's back.
I didn't know to call it foreplay,
But it was foreplay.
And I was pissed.
Why shouldn't I have been pissed?

My cousin was skating with a boy
While Donna Summer was enjoying
A seventeen-minute orgasm.
Little did I know that a seventeen-minute orgasm
Is impossible, or if possible,
Then certainly fatal

For anybody who is not a monk and/or a sex addict.
Jesus, I was twelve or thirteen,
And had become a legendary masturbator.
I was in love with girls and women.
I was in love with the existence
Of girls and women,

And I was desperately in love with my cousin.
So I did what any jealous lover
Of any age has ever done.
I lied. Yes, I clumsily rolled into the middle
Of the rink and told my cousin
That her mother was outside

And was pissed at us for not being ready to go.
        And, ah, my poor cousin, believing me,
                Reluctantly let go
Of that white boy's hand and skated away with me.
        But then that white trash Romeo
                Skated after us,

Spun my cousin around, and tongue-kissed her
        With such force
                That she, as she confessed later,
Almost peed her pants.
        And all of this teenage partial-sex
                Was occurring

While I was enduring Donna Summer
        And her relentless seventeen-minute orgasm?
                Jesus, I pulled my cousin
Away from that boy and, nearly falling,
        Pulled her off the floor
                And into the lobby.

I was so intent on getting her away from the white boy
        That I forget we were still
                Wearing our roller skates,
Until my cousin said, "Our skates, our skates,"
        And turned back toward the rink
                And saw that her white boy

Had already chosen another partner, a white girl,
        And was spinning her around
                In even more complicated circles
As Donna Summer continued to moan and groan
        Her seventeen-minute orgasm.
                I was delighted

That the white trash romancer had been revealed
As yet another 1970s slut-boy,
But my cousin was devastated.
She fell off her skates and landed on her ass
And wept. In public. She wept
In public! Jesus!

Indians are not supposed to weep in public!
There have already been too many
Publicly weeping Indians!
Of course, I didn't say any of that to my cousin.
I didn't want to hurt her.
I wanted to save her.

So I tried to kneel beside her, but fell
Off my skates and landed on her.
She caught me.
She held onto me. She cried into my skinny chest.
She cried out the names
Of the dozen boys

Who had already broken her heart
And I swear she also cried out the names
Of the dozen men
Who would eventually break her heart.
My cousin, sixteen
And aching to be rescued,

Tried to stand. She fell. I fell.
We fell. And I realized
That Donna Summer's seventeen-minute orgasm
Wasn't a disco opera about sex.
It wasn't a song about release.
It was a song about being trapped.

Blood In, Blood Out

Once or twice a day,
White folks dropped their strays
At Little Falls Bay

on the border of our reservation and those orphaned dogs would howl and
chase every passing car and then those dogs would stand at attention and
closely watch but wouldn't chase the passing cars and then those dogs would
lie with heads in paws and follow the passing cars with just their eyes and
then those dogs would slump with their backs to the road and wouldn't even
glance at the passing cars and then those dogs would disappear,

But my family,
With love and mercy,
Rescued two or three

of those sad-ass dogs, including a magical poodle we named Pierre (of course),
and he howled at sirens and he loved us children and he worshipped our
mother and he nearly died from rescued-dog-grief when she was gone to
powwow for two weeks, and he (fixed and sterile) still tried to hump every
four-legged female mammal, and he was ripped in half by another orphaned
dog, an epic St. Bernard, that my big brother adopted despite our objections,

And I, driven mad
With rage, grabbed a bat
And wanted to smash

that St. Bernard in the head and break open its skull and scatter its murderous
brains all over the back porch, but my father, quick and wise, wrestled the
bat from my hands, and saved me from a likely mauling, and my father
held me close as I wept, and ordered my brother to drive that St. Bernard
to the garbage dump and abandon that killer among the old refrigerators,
unrecycled recyclables, and flea-swamped carpets, and let him starve, and my
big brother, weeping for Pierre and the St. Bernard, did as he was told, but
it was not enough justice for me, so I prayed for a week for that St. Bernard's
death, and eight days after he killed Pierre, my family went to the dump, and

we saw the bloated and bloodied body of that St. Bernard, and I celebrated (I danced and sang over the corpse), but that was thirty years ago, and I am now a good father and husband (I hope and believe), and I have become a peaceful man who doesn't believe in violence,

So is it odd
That I still thank God
For killing that dog?

Ceremony

Our mother made rhubarb ice cream
       From the only plant
              In our little reservation town.

Tongue-numbing and too sweet-sharp,
       That rhubarb ice cream
              Knocked us down.

"It's good medicine," our mother said.
       "God gives us the food
              That can save our lives."

We didn't become rhubarb connoisseurs,
       But we ate it, reluctantly,
              With wooden forks and knives.

As children, we resist the ceremonies
       Or the food, familiar and strange,
              That our parents carry.

But if those ceremonies happen to combine
       Food *and* religion, then we cannot
              Be contrary.

So we, through force and choice, came
       To believe that rhubarb was
              Created by God's breath,

And, oh, how we grieved when our neighbor's
       Horses, those four-shoed thieves,
              Stomped that plant to death.

My family has not eaten rhubarb since that day,
       Nor have we spoken in public
              About our sadness.

But we silently rage and rage, having learned
    That food, and the loss of faith,
        Causes madness.

Lamentations

(one)

In 1981, while bicycling to my adopted hometown, I lost
Eighty bucks when I stopped to piss in Reardan Canyon Creek.

(two)

That damn bird, addicted to the color green, picked up
My money and threaded four twenties into her nest.

(three)

My father wrecked twenty-three cars before I was born,
Lost his top teeth in one wreck, and his bottom teeth in another.

(four)

My father only wrecked three cars after my birth.
Why didn't his love for me more often distract him from the road?

(five)

In the absence of manhood ceremonies, American men
Will crash their cars into trees and large bodies of water.

(six)

My eighty bucks fell from that bird's nest and floated downstream
From river to river, and river to ocean, from water to salmon.

(seven)

While eating the best salmon of his life, a man choked
To death on a salt-encrusted twenty-dollar bill.

(eight)

There are three other salmon that remain dangerous
To those of us who don't take small enough bites.

(nine)

My father's love was more dangerous
Than his driving.

(ten)

I have never heroically saved
Anybody from choking to death.

(eleven)

My car is filled with emergency food and water
Because I expect to get trapped by a blizzard.

(twelve)

I also expect to someday fight and kill
Three men who invade my home.

(thirteen)

In the absence of manhood ceremonies, American men
Dream of killing imaginary enemies.

(fourteen)

On the day I lost eighty bucks, I did not eat a thing,
And my father wrecked his car coming to save me.

Unkissed

1.

Who
Knew
The man
Would jackknife,
Leave his lovely wife,
And abandon his preschool kids?
He told me once, "I hate my life." So who knew? I did.

(I am vaguely Catholic, so I am prone to believe that any confession, however casual, is a Holy Confession. Isn't every secret a sacred possession? Shouldn't I honor any intimacy with my silence? Or am I just defending my friend? But, damn, what kind of man leaves his family without kissing them goodbye? And what's more, he left them, not for another woman or man, but for a studio apartment with a big-screen TV. Should I feel guilty for remaining friends with this bastard? These questions are morally complicated, I suppose, or perhaps I'm just being morally relative. Perhaps the question is rather simple: Do I become a liar whenever I conceal the lies of another, no matter how much I love him like a brother?)

2.

"Meet
Me
At noon,"
I said. She
Waited for fifty-
Six minutes then sent me this text:
"I love your forgetful ass but we'll never have sex."

(There was a time, twenty-one years ago, when I romantically loved her—when I drunkenly waded through a shallow pond in my haste to get to her. I could have walked around the water but that would have involved a deviation from a direct line. I pursued her like this despite the fact that she was—and is—a lesbian. Romance has always been impossible. And yet, these days, whenever she flirts, I remember exactly what it felt like to want her so much—to dream of kissing her beneath a streetlight while dozens of unkissed strangers wander past us.)

3.

He's
Free
But served
Thirteen years
For rape and car theft
Before a new DNA test
Exonerated him. He says, "Freedom hurts my chest."

(The prosecuting attorney still believes the right man was convicted. "I have no doubts, none at all," the attorney said to a documentary crew. "And I will go to my grave knowing that a guilty man has been set free." The case depended on eyewitness testimony. The rape victim, an eight-year old girl, first told police that she was attacked by a man who looked like her neighbor. After hours of questioning and coaching, she changed her statement and swore that it was "actually" her neighbor who raped her. Another witness, a different neighbor, swore that he saw the accused man steal a car and race out of the neighborhood. The witness was allowed to make this claim despite the fact that he was extremely nearsighted and was still somehow able to identify the suspect from sixty feet away on a foggy night. The nearsighted man swore that he recognized his neighbor's "eccentric gait." The jury took only three hours to deliver a guilty verdict and the judge sentenced the accused to seventy years. But all of the witnesses—and the arresting officers, prosecuting attorney, jury, and judge—were wrong. They convicted an innocent man. Does that make them liars? Must one lie purposefully in order to be called a liar? Or can a mistake—an accidental misidentification—also be a form of lying? And who do we become when we are confronted with the truth— with a direct refutation of our closely held beliefs—but still refuse to admit to our sins? During a press conference the day after his release from prison, the innocent man swore that he held no grudge. He said he just wanted to get down and kiss the ground—though the ground remained unkissed. He said he forgave everybody and that he wished his best to everybody. But he kept repeating—said it three or four times—that freedom was hurting—was killing—his chest.)

4.

I
Sighed
When she
Passed by my
Desk. She wanted me;
I wanted her. We never kissed.
Twenty years later, I still dream about what I missed.

(She loves her husband and children; I love my wife and boys. I'm not suggesting that I want to change our lives. I don't want to kiss her now— except, I suppose, in my fantasies. But I'm still curious about all the reasons why she and I never acted on our passions. Why didn't we ever take that first step toward removing our clothes? Were we afraid? Were we in denial? Perhaps we just didn't want it enough. Or is there a larger question? Do we become liars when we don't kiss those people who make us tremble and who tremble for us?)

5.

"Whites
Lie!"
My dad
Drunkenly
Shouted to the sky
Then madly climbed into his ride
And promised us that he'd only drink a few. He lied.

(My father, who talked about broken treaties only when he was drinking, died six years ago of alcohol-related kidney failure. But I was not at his bedside. I'd never promised him that I would help him die, so, technically speaking, I didn't lie, but whenever I talk to my mother about my father's death, I have to avert my eyes. I also had to avert my eyes when I first saw my father—no, my father's body—lying in the coffin. My sisters—twins—leaned over to kiss my father, but I could only imagine the coldness, the taste of absence, so I did not kiss him. I only held his hand and only for a moment before I fled back to my chair in the front row where I grieved alone and yet so publicly.)

Web

So many times, my father pawned
His war dance regalia,
And each time, the pawnbroker
Hung the headdress and bustle on his walls
With a "Not For Sale" sign printed
In thick, black ink. I think
The pawnbroker saw more
Beauty in eagle feathers

Than my father did. I think
That broker also saw
More beauty in my father
Than I ever could. The pawn man
Made a living from heartbreak,
But he never sold my father's
War dance. He'd always wait
For my father to find the money

To redeem himself. Now,
Years after his death,
My father's regalia hangs
On my bedroom wall. Yesterday,
I watched a spider crawl
Across the feathers and beads.
I always knew Grief was a storyteller,
But not that it had eight legs.

The Shaman of Ice Cream

"Death is the mother of Beauty."
—Wallace Stevens

Who brings a drum to a funeral?
Who tells dirty jokes?
Who laughs so hard that Diet Pepsi geysers
        out of her nose?
Who brings a drum to a funeral?
Who uses the bacon grease to make fry bread
        and apple pie?
Who puts his hand on his third cousin's thigh?
Who brings a drum to a funeral?
Who asks the Jesuit if he's naked
        beneath his nightgown?
Who uses dynamite to dig a grave
        in the frozen ground?
Who brings a drum to a funeral?
Let this goodbye be Coyote's wet dream.
The only shaman is the shaman of ice cream.

In his coffin, our father is cold to the touch.
He's dead, dead, dead. There is nothing to touch.
His skin is no longer skin.
His eyes are no longer eyes.
His bones are no longer bones.
He is a fossilized hive.
If I picked him up, I could shake him
        like a gourd rattle.
Let this goodbye be a death scream.
The only shaman is the shaman of ice cream.

Traveling

Upon arrival, I collect my baggage
And walk across the bridge

Into the parking structure
Where I discover, to my embarrassment,

That I've been gone too long
And have forgotten where I left my car.

From floor to floor, aisle to aisle,
I walk and walk, searching, searching,

Growing weary and angry. My bags
Are heavy. Too heavy. So I leave them

By an elevator and hope that I find
My car and return to them before

A thief steals them or airport security
Confiscates and destroys what they think

Could be an explosive device. Finally,
I think to look in my wallet

For my parking stub, and I find it,
And yes, I've written down the row

And number, so I rush to that location
And find an unfamiliar car, a small,

Black hatchback that disturbingly
Resembles an insect. This isn't

My car, but I insert my key into the lock,
And it works. So this must be my car.

I take the driver's seat and insert the key
Into the ignition, but the engine will not

Turn, will not turn, will not turn over.
The battery is dead. I have no power.

And then I smell something sweet
And sickening. I know that smell.

It's death. Suddenly terrified, I look
Into the backseat and see what must

Be a body wrapped in garbage bags.
Jesus, Jesus, Jesus, Jesus, Jesus.

I want to run, but I need to know who
Is dead in the backseat of this car

That must not be my car, so I pull back
The garbage bag over the corpse's head

And it's my father, O, God, it's my father.
What is his body doing here? We buried him

Six years ago on the reservation. I threw
A handful of dirt on his coffin, and yet,

Here he is. And his body is strangely
Preserved, as if he had just died yesterday.

And then I am rocked backward when
I notice that my father is breathing

Shallowly. I leap over the seat
And land on my father. I shake and shake

And shake him, but he will not wake.
He will not open his eyes. "Wake up!

Wake up! Wake up! Wake up! Wake up!"
I pound on his chest, on his heart,

And I slap his face and I grab him by
The shoulders and shake, shake, shake him

Until he opens his eyes, barely conscious,
Barely aware, and I scream at him

To come back to me, but he falls
Into sleep, so I punch him in the face,

And bloody his nose, and I punch him
In the gut and hear the air escape his lungs,

And I punch him in the crotch
And that does the trick. My father sits up

Straight and his eyes snap open wide
And he looks at me—he sees me—and he asks,

"Where have you been? Where have you been?"
And I say, "I've been on a trip, a journey

Away from home, but I'm here now, and I am
Not leaving again, and I will stay with you."

And I ask, "But how are you here? How are you
Alive?" And he says, "I don't know, I don't know,"

And then I'm awake. I sit up in bed. It's cold—
Our furnace is too small to properly heat

Our house during a serious freeze. But, wait,
It's not freezing outside. It's unseasonably warm,

And then I realize that somebody—something—
Is in the bedroom with me. I'm alone here

Because my wife is sleeping beside our sick son
In his bedroom. Perhaps our other son has found

His way into this room, but no—something
Large is standing in the corner. Oh, God,

It's a ghost—it's my father's ghost—no,
It's my grief and it opens its mouth

And it wails so loud that it hurts to hear—
My eardrums vibrate—and so I snap on the lamp

And realize that my grief is not standing
In the corner. It's not a ghost, either.

It's a bookshelf. I was frightened by
A bookshelf. This is funny, so I laugh,

And I lie back down, thinking that I might
Find a way back to sleep, but instead,

I weep for my father, I weep for my father.
He's been dead for six years, for six years.

When he died, I cut my long hair.
By custom, I can grow back my hair

When my grief abates, but O, my grief
Floods my bedroom tonight. My bed becomes

A raft and I float up toward the ceiling.
I bump against the ceiling. I am crushed

Against the ceiling and I can't breathe,
I can't breathe, I can't breathe, I can't—

Perhaps I am dying. Perhaps my grief will
Murder me. Perhaps my grief will wrap

My corpse in garbage bags and leave it
In the backseat of a strange car

Parked at the airport. O, I can't breathe,
I can't breathe, as the grief-flood crushes

My lungs against the ceiling. I become
A part of the ceiling. I am the ceiling.

And then, suddenly, I am awake again.
Damn, it was a dream within a dream—

No, a nightmare inside a nightmare—
And I'm sitting on an airplane, weeping.

Beside me, a woman in a business suit
Is also weeping. "Are you okay?"

I ask her. And she smiles and says, "I am
Crying because you were crying in your sleep,

And I couldn't wake you. None of us could
Wake you, and so the pilot is now making

An emergency landing in Pittsburgh.
There will be an ambulance waiting for you."

But I'm awake now, I think, but don't say.
I know I must stop the pilot from landing

This plane, so I race to the cockpit door,
And pound and pound and pound and pound

On the thin metal frame, forgetting we live
In the Age of Terror, and so I have

Unwittingly become a threat to the safety
Of this plane and its passengers, and am

Knocked to the floor and buried beneath
A dozen men, who punch and kick me, who

Gouge my eyes and chew on my fingers and ears.
I don't fight back. I don't fight back.

And then I do fight back. I am suddenly
So strong that nothing can defeat me.

I toss the men aside and I smash through
The cockpit door and I am once again shocked

To see my father, who is now the pilot
Of this plane, and we are plummeting

Toward the ground. "We are going to crash,"
He says. "All of us are going to crash."

And I say, "I know, I know, I know, I know."
And I try to keep my eyes open—I want to see

What happens to us—and as the ground rises
To meet us, I see that it is beautiful—

The world is beautiful. My father is
Beautiful. I am beautiful. Death is

Beautiful. And, O, I lean against
The force of my grief, and I know

That I will wake again. I know this is
A dream—nightmare—but I want to stay

Here for a little while longer. I want
To stay, stay, stay, stay with my father,

My pilot, so I stagger into the empty
Co-pilot's seat, and I take the controls,

And together, my father and I try
To pull us out of this spectacular dive.

Ping-Pong in Rehab

1. It doesn't feel good to skunk a drunk.

2. After I slammed the ball, and hit and killed a moth in mid-flight, my failed-suicide-attempt opponent said it all reminded him of his dead father.

3. A right-handed speed freak killed me while playing with his left hand.

4. There wasn't a budget for extra balls, so when we dented the last one, we just played with it. The random bounces turned it into a different game. We called that game Dead Fathers.

5. During a high-speed match between the two best players, a beautiful anorexic said the blurred paddles and ball looked like a meteor storm flying between two moons.

6. After I slammed the ball into a window, the counselor said, "Don't worry. They're bulletproof." Seeing the look of alarm on my face, she said, "or maybe not."

7. At midnight, the temperature was 101 degrees. The sweat made Rorschach stains on the table. One of them looked like my dead father.

8. Yes, I played against famous addicts. None of them were any good. There's no correlation between perfect pitch and hand-eye coordination.

9. A bipolar woman picked up the paddle, pointed to the empty space beside her, and said, "Do you want to play us doubles?"

10. After I beat her, the bipolar woman asked, "Of course, you know that bipolarism and multiple-personality disorder are very different things?"

11. "Yes, I know they're different," I said. "Do you want to play me and me again?"

12. Insomniacs are often overweight. Instead of sleeping, they eat. One of the best players was an obese dude who hadn't slept a full night in thirty-four

years. He talked about that last good night like other people talk about high school lovers.

13. There were no mosquitoes in that desert. We could play all night and not get bit. "Too bad," the heroin addict said. "I could have pretended they were tiny flying hypodermic needles."

14. Have you ever seen a swarm of mosquitoes drunk on an alcoholic's blood? Flying unsteadily through the dark, they all look like dead fathers.

Downpour

I can't stop writing about my dead father.

He's sixty-two percent of me. Like water.

Come On, Come On, Come On

On the highway,
I pick up a dark passenger.
Will I harm him?
Or will he be my abductor?

He pulls steel
And sharpens it against a stone:
Lies, lies, lies, lies.
Born a twin, but now I'm alone

Or not alone.
I'm the passenger and driver.
I'm the killer,
The weapon, and the survivor.

Honor Song, with Venom

I blast, blast, blast the trumpets and cornets
For you. Listen! I'm a one-man octet.

I'm a fingertip parade. I'm a bum
Knee. I'm a powwow cavalcade of drums

And feathers. I'm bad weather and good sex,
Or vice versa. I'm a tar pit T. Rex.

Am I getting cold? Am I getting warm?
I'm a hornet, in love, ready to swarm.

Lean Cuisine

The best meal that I ever ate
Was in an ancient fishing village
On the Spanish Mediterranean coast.

Fresh tomato on still-warm bread slathered with garlic,
And baby fish, bones and all, caught that morning.

As I ate, I kept thinking, "I might be the only
Native American who has ever eaten baby fish,
Bones and all, in an ancient fishing village
On the Spanish Mediterranean coast."

Forget Neil-goddamn-Armstrong!
Every Indian has been the only Indian somewhere.
Every Indian has been the First Man on the Moon.

But I digress. So let me repeat:

The best meal that I ever ate
Was in an ancient fishing village
On the Spanish Mediterranean coast.

Fresh tomato on still-warm bread slathered with garlic,
And baby fish, bones and all, caught that morning.

To confess, I ate dozens of baby fish, bones
And all, and enough bread to make two loaves.

Gluttony, thy name is Sherman, bones and all.

After the meal, I drank coffee
As strong and bitter as colonialism.

And I, through my translator friend, asked
The restaurant owner/chef if
A Native American, a Red Indian, had
Ever eaten there, and he said, in Spanish,

"Of course, of course, my great-grandfather
Was honored to serve Sitting Bull."

Holy shit, I thought.

Sitting Bull!
Sitting Bull!
Sitting Bull, bones and all!
Santa mierda, I thought.
Suddenly, I was Buzz
Aldrin, Second Man
On the Moon. Suddenly,
Every Indian was potentially
The Second Man on the Moon.

O, I swooned. Who knew?

There might be six degrees of
Separation among all white folks,
But between Indians, there's only two,
Even on the Spanish Mediterranean coast.

Who knew? Did you?

O, sing an honor song,
Sing an honor song
For baby fish, bones and all!

But, damn, it wasn't fair,
For I was too fat to sing,
So I eased my belt,
And leaned back in my chair,
My belly warm and full
With the same meal
That had pleased Sitting Bull.

Salvation

Whatever happened to that pretty Jehovah's Witness
      Who used to visit me?
Red hair and blue jeans. She stood at my front door
      And proselytized a bit,
But mostly she talked about how much she wanted
      To leave that little
College town. And though I did see her around
      That town—at the grocery store,
The coffee shop, and ice cream shop—we never
      Spoke away from my door.
When I asked her why not, she said she didn't want
      To embarrass me in front
Of my friends, and I was afraid of how much
      I wanted to be her possession,
Her particular sinner. Of course, there's a long
      History of indigenous boy
And white girl romances. It's a mandatory part
      Of colonialism, but I like
To think I wanted her because she was smart
      (She worked as a biology
Lab assistant) and ambitious (she wanted to live
      In Seattle, which seemed
At the time like the world's largest metropolis
      To both of us) and suspicious
Of her elders (as I have always been). But I suspect
      I wanted her for the oldest reason:
To get revenge on all the white men who dehumanized
      Me. And I suspect
She wanted me for the exact same reason. But we
      Never so much as shook hands,
And I graduated and left town without saying
      Goodbye. I worry
That she still lives there. I worry that she married
      A man chosen by her parents.
I worry that she has become an atheist forced

To spend endless hours
In church. And I wonder if she ever thinks of me.
        Does she even remember
The Indian boy who didn't believe a word
        She said about God, but
Believed every word she said about loneliness
        And the gradual loss of hope?

Sonnet, with Rick Springfield

1. I once made a mix tape that was sixty minutes of "Jesse's Girl." 2. God, I miss cassette tapes. I miss the hiss of unrequited love. 3. I miss being fourteen and in love with, yes, my best friend's girlfriend. 4. I was in love with her at fifteen, sixteen, seventeen, eighteen, and nineteen, as well. I was in love with her for years after she broke up with my best friend. 5. When I was twenty, and drinking my way into blackouts, I called her house. I was too scared to talk to my beloved, who was away at college, but I needed to confess to her mother. 6. But her father answered. It was four in the morning. 7. "I'm in love with your daughter," I said. 8. "We know," he said. He was amazingly polite despite the fact that I'd woken him at dawn-thirty. He said, "You got lucky. She's here for the weekend. You want to talk to her?" 9. I'm an indigenous American who has been in romantic love with half a dozen white women. 10. And only one Indian woman. 11. And yet, I think of my Indian wife and I as loving like Romeo and Juliet. Because I grew up on one reservation as a tribal boy and she lived on a dozen reservations as the daughter of a Bureau of Indian Affairs superintendent. 12. If you don't understand that conflict, then you just need to know that the BIA was originally located in the War Department. 13. I was one year sober when I met my wife. I've been sober ever since. 14. Drunk for the white girls; sober for the Indian woman. Somebody needs to write a song about that.

Hunger

My aunt said, "I remember when your family
First traveled from the reservation
To visit us here in Seattle. Your big brother—
He must have been seven or eight
At the time—wanted to go see a movie,
But I said we didn't have any money,
And he said, 'Well, just do what my Mom
And Dad do, sell the furniture, and move
Into a motel in Spokane'"

Of course, we laughed—
It's a funny story—but the tip of my nose
Went numb. If scent, as they say, is the primary
Sense of memory, then I guess memory
Had deadened my nerves. As much as I remember
Being at the mercy of poor and drunk
And impulsive parents, I often forget
Certain details. I obviously need to forget

Such things. Driving home that night, my wife
Asked me if I remembered living in a motel.
I said, "I know that we lived in a lot
Of dirty motels, but I'd forgotten my parents
Once sold our furniture because we were so broke,
And moved us into a horrible Spokane hotel
So we could qualify for food bank charity.
But I do remember they'd bring back cardboard boxes

Filled with canned goods, and we kids would
Get so excited because there was always something
Different to eat. I think we thought our parents
Were bringing us buried treasure." That night,

As my wife and sons slept, I sat in the dark
With a can of soup—my talisman—and prayed

That my sons would never know even one hungry day.

Creation Story

Lust-drunk, on-the-clock fertile, and married,
My wife and I conceived two gorgeous sons.
But in between those births, she miscarried
A third child, a star of cells too young

To be gendered. We'd wanted a girl,
So we choose to mourn an unborn daughter
By keeping her birth announcements furled
And unread. But wait, I am the father—

No, the poet—no, the mad scientist
Who needs to reanimate blood and flesh.
I am God! I am God! I am Genesis!
I can bring my daughter back from the dead!

(Of course that's not true. This is just a poem.)

But I hope our lost daughter becomes more
Than a father's blasphemous metaphor.

Love Story, without Firewood

A reservation Indian boy, I lived without indoor water until I was
      seven years old.

A white archaeologist, as skinny and old as his dinosaur bones, had
      donated thousands of unsold *National Geographic* 'zines
      to the rez library, so we boldly burned those to battle the cold.

Once, I imagined and traced a lovely Indian woman's face in the ice
      frozen to the inside of our kitchen window.

I never met that imaginary Indian woman, of course, but I did meet a
      Hidatsa Indian woman during a blizzard, fierce and sub-zero.

Over the centuries, how many Indians, subsistence-living, have fallen,
      hungry and poor, and died in the ice and snow?

Now married for seventeen years, that Hidatsa and I, trapped by a
      hundred-year storm on a Seattle freeway with other cold-shocked
      urban souls,
            laughed and kissed to stay warm, waltzed in our seats
               to an old song on the radio, then abandoned
                  the car and walked safely home.

One Marriage, Three Airports or
One Airport, Three Marriages

1.

The man in front of me has missed his flight,
So he throws his passport to the carpet.
He'll be sleeping in Motel 6 tonight.
The man in front of me has missed his flight
Because he thought that he had enough time
To make that last connection to Charlotte.
The man in front of me has missed his flight
And he dreads the reaction from his wife.

2.

At the X-ray machine, the wife removes
One shoe and reveals her left big toe
Poking out of her sock. It's killer-cute.
At the X-ray machine, that wife removes
Her left sock. And her good husband approves.
"Such gorgeous feet," he says to her and, oh,
To the X-ray machine. That wife removes
Her shoes and socks to go where beauty goes.

3.

To be safe, they fly on different planes
When they travel away from their two boys.
It's superstitious and a touch insane,
But it's safer to fly different planes
Through separate lighting, thunder, and rain.
After all, planes were first built to destroy.
To be safe, they fly on different planes
And enjoy their briefly separate fates.

146

Steel Anniversary

1.

In this life, I have loved six women.

I have seen five dogs get crushed to death by cars.

Four of those women have loved me back.

Or maybe it's three.

Two of those dogs were mine.

One of those women, I married.

2.

If I could only read one book for the rest of my life, I would
        choose it randomly.

If I could only read two books for the rest of my life, one of them
        would be about outdoor survival techniques.

Back in high school, after I'd had sex for only the third time, I
        totaled my car when I hit and killed a deer.

It had four legs, of course, and four antler prongs.

During his life, my big brother has hit and killed five deer.
        And totaled five cars.

I'm terrified that the sixth will take his life.

3.

When I asked my wife what she thinks of when she hears the number six,
      she said, "Julius Erving's basketball number."

My wife has five siblings. Her big sister played college basketball.

During this poem, I will tell four lies.

Lie #3: My wife doesn't know Julius Erving's number. But I put those
      words into her mouth to demonstrate her beauty and intelligence.
      Or maybe it's something more sinister. Would I love my wife more
      if she could instantly recall Dr. J's number?

If my wife could only read two books during her lifetime, she would
      choose The Bible, New American Version, and a theological tome
      by her latest favorite Jesuit.

I asked her, "Do you think there's one God?" She said, "There's one God
      expressed in innumerable ways."

4.

One god appears to me in the form of a waterproof, quilted ice
      scraper mitten.

Another god created man in his own image; therefore, that god has
      a receding hairline.

However, the God of Hair gave my wife and me these epic tresses;
      our love story is told by long, black hair scripting every
      surface of our home.

I pray that a vengeful god drops meteors on the speeding drivers who
      killed my dogs.

God's favorite book is his ghost-written autobiography.

Since a good education depends on a low student-teacher ratio,
        I think each god should only be allowed six believers.

5.

I have the blood of six tribes.

My wife has the blood of five.

When I was four, I was an epileptic. When my wife was four,
        she was hiding in the closet during her father's drunken rages.

Our third child should have been a daughter, but she was miscarried.
        My wife and I sometimes sit in the dark and tell each other stories
        about our daughter's imaginary life.

We have two sons. Their favorite hero is Luke Skywalker, who grew
        up on a planet with two suns. I don't believe in magic, but I believe
        in interpreting coincidence exactly the way you want to.

When I ask my sons if they believe in one god, they say,
        in unison, "Huh?"

6.

"You got one lifetime, dude. Fill it up."

I've heard the above statement said by two different men in two
        very different circumstances.

I Google searched "I will love you for three lifetimes," thinking that
        an ancient Chinese poet must have written some version of that
        line, but I only found repeated references to Dolly Parton's classic
        song, "I Will Always Love You," or to Whitney Houston's bipolar
        cover version of the same tune.

Given the choice, we'd all choose wives who were more like Dolly
Parton than Whitney Houston. Hell, we'd choose husbands who
were more Dolly than Whitney. As the ancient Chinese poet wrote,
"You will meet your true love during your fourth reincarnation.
If you fuck it up, you'll have to start all over."

My wife and I have been in love for so long that our first-date
movie tickets cost only five dollars each.

Sweetheart, look into the sky. If I were a god, I'd build six
constellations for you: The Daughter, Deer, Dog, Julius Erving,
and Two Sons Linked.

The Naming Ceremony

My Indian name is Secret,
So let me share it with you.
My Indian name is Two Dogs Fucking,
But no, that's not true.
That's only the punch line to an old joke.
My Indian name is Old Joke.
My Indian name is Fish Bone Choke,
So that means my spirit animal is
Dr. Henry Heimlich.
My Indian name is Bear Hug.
My Indian name is Magic Trick.
My Indian name is Navajo Rug,
Though I'm not Navajo.
My Indian name is Not Navajo.
My Indian name is Turquoise
Is Only A Pretty Rock Among My People.
My Indian name is Afraid Of Church Steeples.
My Indian name is Hobson's Choice,
Which means you either take what's offered
Or you get nothing at all.
My Indian name is Takes Nothing.
My Indian name is Takes All.
My Indian name is Little Falls,
After the Spokane River dam located
On the border of my reservation.
That dam was once the largest in the world,
But it's now smaller than any Ikea.
My Indian name is Assemble Your Own Furniture.
My Indian name is Ecological Preservation.
Ha, ha, ha, ha, oh, brother,
I'm full of shit.
I'm named after my mother,
Who was known as Woman Who Dumps Peanuts
Into Her Diet Pepsi, Takes One Drink,
And Throws The Can Out The Car Window

High Speed Into The Ditch.
We just call her Peanuts for short.
My Indian name is Little Peanuts.
My Indian name is Man Named After A Woman.
My Indian name is Simultaneously In Love With
And Afraid Of The Matriarchy.
My Indian name is Ungrateful Son.
My Indian name is Temperamental Brother.
My Indian name is Distant Uncle.
My Indian name is Rodeo Buckle,
Though I have never ridden a horse,
Of course, because I'm not that kind of Indian.
My Indian name is Not That Kind Of Indian.
My Indian name is Pawn Shop
Because I bought my rodeo buckle
In Dutch's Pawn Shop in downtown Spokane.
My Indian name is Pawned Wedding Ring.
My Indian name is Doesn't Sing.
My Indian name is Doesn't Dance.
My Indian name is Pongs But Won't Ping.
My Indian name is Hate At First Glance,
Which seems like a cynical name,
I know, but damn, I'm an Indian,
So why should I trust anybody,
Especially other Indians?
My Indian name is Trust No One.
My Indian name is Fox.
My Indian name is Fuck Your Cotillion.
My Indian name is Worth Millions,
Though, in fact, I'm only land rich,
Being part owner, along with my siblings,
Of a thousand acres of reservation wheat land
That we lease to gentleman farmers.
My Indian name is Only Land Rich.
My Indian name is Not A Gentleman Farmer.
My Indian name is Afraid Of Barbers,
Because I don't like to have my hair cut,
Though I've been going to the same guy

For eighteen years.
How do I explain that?
Well, he's not a barber,
He's a hair stylist.
My Indian name is Obsessed With Hair.
My Indian name is Defined By Hair.
My Indian name is Reservation Kiss,
Which, unlike the French variety,
Means you kiss without tongue.
But, wait, I must confess.
There is no such thing as the reservation kiss.
I made it up.
I can make up any shit about Indians
And you will believe me
Because you don't know shit about Indians,
Or rather, all you know is bullshit
About Indians, so I can just make up
My own bullshit and you won't know
The difference.
My Indian name is Perennial Bullshitter,
Or as my spell corrector would have it:
Perennial Bulls Hitter.
Bull hitting is an ancient and sacred tradition
Among my tribe.
It's a dangerous manhood ceremony.
The warrior must wait
Until a bull has mounted a cow,
And then must race to the bovine couple
And slap the thrusting bull across the face.
My Indian name is Dash Across The Field
While Dodging Steaming Cow Pies.
My Indian name is Jumps Fences.
My Indian name is Can't Wear Contact Lenses.
My Indian name is Hair Of The Dog.
My Indian name is Hair Of The God.
My Indian name is Two Cows Fucking,
But no, that's not true.
That's only the punch line to a new joke.

My Indian name is New Joke.
My Indian name is Secondhand Smoke.
My Indian name is Wants To Tell You
His Indian Name Because It Makes Him Feel
More Indian.
My Indian name is More Or Less Indian.
My Indian name is Moniker,
Which could be defined as a tautology,
An unnecessary repetition of meaning
Using different words,
Which, if you already knew the meaning
Of tautology means that I might be practicing
A form of tautology by defining it for you.
But, dang, that's all tangential.
My Indian name is Pretty Tangential,
So let me get back to the original point:
Considering that the word *moniker*
Probably comes from the Irish,
It is pretty damn funny
For an Indigenous American to be called
By an Irish name.
My Indian name is Danny Boy.
My Indian name is Paddy O'Brien.
My Indian name is Where
Are The Goddamn Potatoes?
My Indian name is Sherman Alexie,
Which is a ridiculous name
For an Indian, to be sure,
Considering that Alexie is
Usually a Russian first name,
And a sherman is,
In Old English,
A sheep cart driver.
So, according to my Indian name,
I am a shepherd from Vladedivacistan.
My Indian name is Not A Communist.
My Indian name is Not A Red Red.
My Indian name is Souvenir Bobblehead.

My Indian name is Sherman Alexie, Jr.
Yes, if you can believe it,
There are two Indians in the world
Named Sherman Alexie,
Though one of us is dead.
My Indian name is My Name Is
On A Gravestone.
My Indian name is Would Rather Be Alone.
My Indian name is Giving The Dog A Bone.
My Indian name is Giving The God A Bone.
My Indian name is Drum Solo.
My Indian name is Won't Wear A Bolo
Because I don't like to dress like a typical Indian,
And by that, I mean like a typical American male.
Oh, I used to dress like one,
But then, in a rental car shuttle,
I noticed that every man, whether white, black,
Or me, was wearing khaki pants
And a blue button-down shirt.
My Indian name is Yeah, Steve McQueen
Looked Great In Khakis And A Blue Shirt,
But That Doesn't Mean You Do, Too.
My Indian name is Phillips Screwdriver,
Because I remember the clever story,
Written by an old-friend-turned-stranger,
About a man who wanders his world
And, using a screwdriver, slightly loosens
Every screw he can find.
I never actually read the story.
I'm not sure my old friend ever wrote
The story, or if
It was only an idea,
A story yet to be purchased
And assembled at your local Ikea.
But, man, oh, man, over the years,
I've often wanted to write my own version
Of that story.
I never have, and likely never will,

But I confess

That I have dreamed of being a literary thief.

My Indian name is Always In Grief.

My Indian name is Been To A Hundred Funerals.

My Indian name is Sick Of Wakes.

My Indian name is Medium Rare Steaks.

My Indian name is Hit The Brakes

Because the truth is

That I have no Indian name.

My Indian name is Unnamed.

My Indian name is Unclaimed.

My Indian name is Without Flame.

My Indian name is Lame.

But wait, no, I'm lying again.

My Indian name is Lies, Lies, Noun And Verb.

My Indian name is Do Not Disturb.

My Indian name is Bitterroot.

My Indian name is Secret,

So let me share it with you.